Abram Newkirk Littlejohn

Individualism

Its Growth and Tendencies, with some Suggestions as to the Remedy for its Evils ;

Sermons Preached Before the University of Cambridge in November, 1880

Abram Newkirk Littlejohn

Individualism
Its Growth and Tendencies, with some Suggestions as to the Remedy for its Evils ; Sermons Preached Before the University of Cambridge in November, 1880

ISBN/EAN: 9783337084578

Printed in Europe, USA, Canada, Australia, Japan

Cover: Foto ©Thomas Meinert / pixelio.de

More available books at **www.hansebooks.com**

INDIVIDUALISM:

ITS GROWTH AND TENDENCIES:

WITH SOME SUGGESTIONS AS TO

THE REMEDY FOR ITS EVILS.

SERMONS PREACHED BEFORE THE UNIVERSITY
OF CAMBRIDGE IN NOVEMBER, 1880.

BY THE RIGHT REVEREND

A. N. LITTLEJOHN, D.D., LL.D.,
BISHOP OF LONG ISLAND.

Cambridge:
DEIGHTON, BELL AND CO.
LONDON: GEORGE BELL AND SONS.
NEW YORK: T. WHITTAKER.
1881

CONTENTS.

SERMON I.

INDIVIDUALISM : ITS GROWTH AND TENDENCIES.

GENERAL aim of these Sermons—The status of the Individual in ancient life—His status in modern life—The vast change—Christianity preeminently influential in effecting it—The three periods in the history of Individualism—Causes which, in our time, have stimulated the growth of Individualism—Diffusion of political power—Advance of knowledge—Rapid growth of wealth—Enlarged control of the powers of nature—The age one of transition—Consequent instability of popular convictions, and detachment of the Individual from the settled traditions of the past—The Individual reason lifted more and more into the place of the collective, continuous judgment of mankind—Tendencies (1) as seen in the character of individuals and in the general character of the time—(2) Their influence on Morality—(3) Their influence as it affects the Faith, Ordinances, Worship and Polity of the Church—(4) Their influence hostile to the Traditions of the race—(5) Have helped to establish the absolutism of Public Opinion—(6) In sympathy with the two leading phases of Modern Socialism—(7) The tendencies of Individualism illustrated by the present condition and prospects of the Art-work, the Art-impulse of the time.

SERMON II.

INDIVIDUALISM : COUNTER TRUTHS.

The duty devolved upon the teachers and representatives of Christianity—The difficulty and urgency of the Church's work in dealing with the problems presented by the threatened excess of

SERMON III.

INDIVIDUALISM:
INSTITUTIONAL CHECKS AND LIMITATIONS.

SERMON I.

PSALM VIII. 1, 3, 4, 5, 6.

O Lord our Governor, how excellent is thy name in all the earth!......When I consider thy heavens, the work of thy fingers, the moon and the stars, which thou hast ordained; What is man, that thou art mindful of him? and the son of man, that thou visitest him? For thou hast made him a little lower than the angels, and hast crowned him with glory and honor. Thou madest him to have dominion over the works of thy hands; thou hast put all things under his feet.

THIS Psalm, in magnifying God's glory by His works and by His love to man, describes the latter as he was originally created, and as he will be again when the Mediatorial work of Christ shall be accomplished. Though every man's probation may be complete in

L. S.   1 itself, yet the result of it, as exhibited in the average character of the individual, is still only the prophecy, not the verification, of his promised oneness with God and the consequent restoration of his lost perfection. However far he may be from the final goal, it is certain that he has grown to be a much larger figure than he once was, as compared with the bulk of human life, or with the life of institutions ordained of God for his guidance and discipline. On all sides the individual has been so much widened and deepened as, now and then, to tempt him to question the lawful authority of those institutions.

In other times the origin, the mutual relations, the rightful functions of the Family, the State, and the Church have been abundantly discussed. But now there are many circumstances, of which none can be ignorant, which prove that the time has come when we must give, not less thought, indeed, to these forms of organic life, but more to the individual. His relations to the external powers working upon him are gradually shifting, and in such ways as to assure him of a constantly increasing prominence in the future. It is of moment, therefore, that we should seek to define, as clearly as possible, his due place and influence, to restore where it has been lost, and to preserve where it still exists, the equilibrium between his own life and a life larger than his own.

The development of the individual has been at once a cause and an effect of the progress of the race. The two facts have been correlative and inseparable. In the early stages of society and even in the most advanced ones of the ancient life there was no true idea of man, as man. "He belonged not to himself and had no independent, substantive existence*." The monarch owned the subject, the father the son, the husband the wife, the master the slave; and so absolute was the ownership that it excluded even the vaguest notion of the *jus naturale* of the individual, as we understand it. Everywhere and in all relations "he was simply the function of another's will, the appendage to outward authority." If his life or his property was wanted for any purpose whether of war, or of peace, or for the altars of religion, both were taken without a thought of wrong. And when all might be taken what was left was regarded in the light of a concession or privilege. The patriarch's only struggle when about to sacrifice Isaac was with

* See opening pages of Dr Mozley's "Ruling Ideas," &c.

1—2

natural affection, not with any scruples as to his right to do so. "That children should share their parent's guilt and punishment was recognized by the civil law of all ancient Eastern life as a sound judicial principle." Sparta did not hesitate to destroy the infirm infants born within its borders, but considered itself as having an unchallenged right to do as it pleased in this and in all kindred matters involving the disposal of human life. Even Roman law, so much lauded for its enlightened spirit in dealing with personal property, never rose above the average pagan idea in regard to the higher question of the ownership of man by man. Such was the fact, and the other noteworthy fact going with it was that no form of the ancient life had in itself any available power to make it otherwise. Neither its religious, nor its social organizations, nor its political policies formally and consciously attempted to do so. The last chapters of the old Asiatic and of the old Greek and Roman civilizations closed with substantially the same teaching and the same practice on this subject as had been exhibited by the earliest. Now if we were required to name the one most salient and characteristic difference between the ancient and the modern life, we should undoubtedly find it in their respective notions as to the individuality of man. A vast change has been accomplished, and, whatever other agencies may have cooperated to bring it about, Christianity, beyond all question, supplied the principles that originated it and the most potent of the instrumentalities by which those principles were enabled, however slowly, to assert their practical supremacy. To show how Christianity achieved this greatest of revolutions would be to describe Christianity itself—its view of man as made in the image of God, the seminal principle of our substantive, human personality—its doctrine of God in Christ coming in the fulness of time to recover the lost glory of that image by making man a partaker of His own life, and so an heir of immortality—its offer of redemption to all men without respect of persons or of the accidents of human lot—its message of universal brotherhood resting upon the revealed purpose of God that all men should be gathered into one fold and under one Shepherd—its declaration of a judgment to come wherein every man will be judged according to his work ; and, finally, its own life-power from whatever source drawn, incorporated into a visible, historic

kingdom, and through that moving upon the king-
doms of this world and leavening all social and
political institutions : not scattering the truths
entrusted to it at random as winds and waters
scatter the seed thrown out upon them; but sending
them out from its own heart in well defined and
orderly currents of power, through the lips of duly
commissioned ministers, through offices of worship,
through Sacraments and a positive discipline over
human wills and consciences. It was not the Gospel
merely as truth, or spirit, or energy, or influence, but
the embodied Gospel, Christianity organized, the
very Church of the living God that, in respect of the
great principle of man's individuality, lifted the world
"into another orbit and rolled it along another
course." I emphasize the fact in this connection for
a reason that will be seen further on. The individual is no larger to day in the estimation of
Christianity, than he was when it first began to
propagate the principles that, more than all else,
have made man what he is in modern society. For
well nigh eighteen centuries it preached and
laboured to accomplish this, among other and, in
view of eternity, more important results; but it has

been only within the present century that our civilization has accepted it in its integrity, and then only after revolutions and upheavals which shook modern life to its centre. This gradual falling into line with Christianity—this slowly developed and now almost complete accord with the Church respecting the intrinsic value and self-centred life of the individual is now the vaunted characteristic of the more advanced social and political ethics of our time. The thought and practice, however, of the leading races of the world to-day have yet scarcely labored up to the original standpoint of the Church of Christ. It is beginning to be seen and to be generally admitted that the more aggressive, if not the more highly developed forms of modern life, are democratic in their tendency. What is yet only a tendency in England and in most other countries of the Continent is an accomplished fact among fifty millions of people across the sea. The genius and aims of Democracy may, in some quarters, excite grave apprehension and very justly, because, like all new forces, it will be inclined to extremes and develop more or less licence and disorder. But at its core one great idea is planted, one great impulse is

struggling for mastery; and that idea is the majesty
of the individual—that impulse is to make the most
of the individual. What history proves to be true of
every principle that has acquired a more or less
durable sovreignty over mankind in any sphere of
life, will no doubt prove true of the Democratic
principle. Long checked, repressed, often crushed by
institutions and organizations which, however un-
wisely administered, always recognized as part of
their *raison d'être* the education of man as man, the
individual has at last moved up to the front and is
rapidly advancing toward a position where he will be
strongly tempted to overrate himself, and corre-
spondingly to underrate what is external to himself,
whether it be the truth and grace of God, or the
established institutions of Society, the State and the
Church. One period in the history of Individualism—
that of its outgrowth, is now well nigh finished. To
this will succeed that of its exaggeration—the period
which, if not coincident with, at least overlaps the
present generation. After this will follow the period
of distortion and abuse running out, at last, into
eclipses of reason and conscience, and into disruptions
and anarchies of every name; and finally into reac-

tions toward a recovery of the lost balance between the personal and impersonal, the subjective and objective, the individual and the organic body whether social, political, or ecclesiastical. Now if it be true that our time is to witness the exaggeration of the relative importance of the individual, it is of grave moment that we should watch closely this drift of the age, and examine under the best light we have not only the evident symptoms of its power, but also some of the more unwholesome fruits which it has already produced : and then if we can, indicate the remedy.

Whatever these fruits are, we should not be surprised at them. Their growth has been neither sudden nor mysterious. Causes have been at work to produce them which lie out on the surface of life. What wonder that the individual should be tempted into undue self-assertion, when we consider how many things have helped to exalt him in his own estimation. The wider and wider diffusion of political power has taught him that the ballot is mightier than the bayonet and that rulers and parliaments can no longer permanently resist his will. Knowledge has rapidly advanced, and the misfortune is that he has just enough of it to engender pride and not enough to teach humility. Wealth, too, has grown so fast as to breed a greedy lust for the power which it creates, as well as a passionate thirst for the comfort and ease that follow in its wake. While physical science has turned over to him without reserve or qualification its own immensely enlarged control of nature's powers. But stronger, perhaps, than anything else working in this direction is the now popular view of the age as one of flux and transition. Apparently, nothing is sure of continuing long in one stay. It is said that we are breaking away from the old anchorages, and that the new ones have not yet been found. A "thaw", we are told, has begun in Theology which threatens to relax its joints and to resolve its positive elements into a shifting vapour of sentiment, replacing, as its final result, all definite beliefs with certain vague aspirations after a truth about God and duty that will be so large and free as to spurn the trammels of formula. Not a few, too, as we have been reminded, of the old religious and ethical traditions, which we had supposed to be so permanently imbedded in the consciousness of mankind, as to be lifted above the eddies of change, have been summoned to the bar of inquiry, and questioned in a way that implies a distrust of their supremacy, and a disposition to modify, if not overthrow their influence. Indeed, there are certain leaders of the thought of our day whose speculations have acquired a singular charm over the popular mind, who, either out of charity towards our weakness, or courtesy toward prejudices that have not ceased to be respectable, tell us that, amid the attempted reconstruction of the very foundations of human knowledge now going on, these venerable heirlooms of faith and duty are destined to take their place among the exploded conceits of the race. And then, as part and parcel of the same drift, we are told that not only do the Family, the State, and the Church exist for the benefit of the individual, and in his advancing power and glory, find the only power and glory which they can legitimately claim: but, what is a far more radical and disturbing idea, that they have no divine and unchangeable principles of organization; but, like all lower forms of corporate life, are to be dealt with as the accidental and ever mutable embodiments of the social instincts of man. And, further, coupled with this drift, nay, as an inevitable

effect of it, there is the notion that the only court
of appeal, in determining the character and extent of
these revisions and amendments, is not the collective,
continuous judgment of mankind, nor any standard
above and outside the individual; but each man's
reason working out the problems for and by itself.
It matters not how this new gospel reaches the
masses, whether as science or philosophy, as poetry
or fiction, as the culture that dilutes our God and
Father into "a power that makes for righteousness,"
or as the barren visions of agnostic dreamers, the
effect is all one way.   The individual emerges more
and more as the central figure.   At first, dazed somewhat, it may be, by so flattering an estimate of his
capabilities, he seems a little chary of accepting the
proffered honor with its inseparable risks.   But pride
has never yet failed to get the better of humility
in the average man.   The temptation to play the
sovereign in the world of intellect, and in the yet
higher one of morals and religion is too alluring
to be resisted: and in a sense not dreamed by the
poet his self-confidence will soon learn to affirm with
easy complacency,

Nil mortalibus arduum est.

But however imperfectly I may have accounted for the Individualistic tendency of the day, the fact of its increasing prominence will not be questioned. Interesting as it may be to explain the fact, it is of more importance to trace the evidences of its power, to sift the good from the evil in the mixed harvest to be reaped from its sowing, and to ascertain what are the available safeguards against its excesses.

(I) And first let us note how this tendency works itself out, in a twofold way, in the character of individuals and in the general character of the time. Both exhibit traits which, though widely contrasted on the surface, are the offspring of the same causes. If I accept the current judgment of the most eminent critics, I must speak of them, on the one side, as unheroic, easily drawn into compromises and weak assents, as full of moral and intellectual indecision, as without stability or earnestness of convictions, and, in the most serious and profound concerns of life, as lethargic and indifferent. And they are so because their thinking is of the same tone: and what else could be their *thinking* when it is so widely the *feeling* of men that there is nothing sure but doubt, nothing certain but change, nothing real but what the senses can discern, nothing of value that does not tell upon the welfare of the individual; and, further still, what else could be the dominant feeling when the individual mind finds in self-guidance, self-sufficiency, self-laudation, self-pleasing the chief articles of its faith. Moral greatness cannot thrive in such an atmosphere. The first condition of growing heroic souls is forgetfulness of self. The self-conscious man is cursed with the feebleness of a low, as well as a narrow motive. The energy that moves him may be intense, but it is the energy that exhausts itself on the aims of the ambitious schemer, the money maker, the pleasure seeker, the worldling of any and every name. This, however, is no more the energy that lifts souls into the higher life whose doing and suffering are recognized as the chief treasures of the race, than water is blood. The one is quite equal to the task of making, but not to the task of bearing the cross. This is the one side. If now we look at the other side, we shall find the average character of the individual and of the age exhibiting qualities so opposite to these, that, at first thought, we can scarcely credit their existence. We have only to shift the point of view and the doubt vanishes. The same character, that, looked at from one direction, seems to be lacking in heroic impulse, to be vague of purpose, weak in will-power, careless, unenthusiastic, at peace because there is nothing important enough to quarrel about: regarded from another, is found to be headstrong and belligerent in pushing its rights, aggressive and even revolutionary in its theories, protestant and inquisitive in its literature, disquieted and restive in temper as though a very fever were raging in its blood, and abounding in rapid transitions and continual surprises.

Now the mystery of the contrast, if not the contrast itself, disappears, when we trace it to its source. Here, again, Individualism comes to the front. Its power tells on both aspects of character, as well in what it does, as in what it leaves undone. On the one hand, it chills and impoverishes character, robs it of fervor, depth, decision, sympathy, trust; and does it in, at least, these two ways—by detaching man more and more from the contact and sway of organic institutions framed to give due scope and poise to his faculties, and next by subjecting his inherited ethical and religious beliefs to the unstable and often capricious handling of the individual reason. On the other hand, it inspires character with the spirit of unrest and belligerency by teaching man that himself individually considered, should be the sole object of solicitude in Society, in the State, and the Church; that he has more rights than he has ever claimed; that among these is the yet only half asserted right to frame his own ideal of what the world ought to be in its relations to himself and to regard the non-fulfilment of that ideal as a personal grievance to be redressed by incessant agitation and attack upon the existing order of things: that it is part of his duty to be on the watch for something to strike rather than for something to defend; that unless he would let the true spirit of manhood die out of him he must be somewhere and in some form an avenger and an iconoclast; that it is treason to his future as well as a base veneration for the dead past to seem to be satisfied with what *is*. Thus it is the tendency of Individualism to unsettle the foundations and to mar the symmetry of character. Under its sway character so far from being what it ought to be—the balanced and orderly result of the means provided by Divine Wisdom and by the long ages of human experience for the training of man, dwindles gradually into a lopsided embodiment of the reigning theories, the master passions, and the ever-shifting aims of the hour.

It is the supreme purpose of Christian discipline, as the crown and perfection of all culture, to build up character into completeness, not so much by displacing the outward law of righteousness, as by clothing character with the unity and steadiness, the strength and continuity of the law itself. But it is the inevitable effect of this high-wrought conception of the individual to reverse this aim by constantly adding to the caprices and instabilities of human life. Parted from its normal centres of outward control, loosed from the bands thrown around it by the enduring organisms of society civil and ecclesiastical, it fluctuates with every tide of impulse, nay with every wave of speculation that strikes it.

I have spoken of the influence of Individualism on two leading phases of character. There is still another which it affects, if possible, still more disastrously. In the Christ-like type of character, the virtues are so grouped as to lift the passive above the active ones—submission, patience, fortitude, humility, self-sacrifice, above the qualities which develop push and energy, resistance, enterprise, aggression, self-assertion. This is simply a fact of the Gospel. I am not concerned here with the Christian philosophy that underlies it; nor do I care to defend it against adverse criticism. We are quite familiar with what certain thinkers say about it, and with the world's general conception of it. I name it only to show how the Christian ideal of character is disparaged and disrupted by the tendency of thought and action now under consideration.

The Christian ideal never treats the individual apart from a life larger than his own. It may be the life of the Family, the life of Society, the life of the Race, the life of the Church, the life of God. It teaches the individual that he can find his true life only by losing it in a life greater than his own. It puts him under a discipline of self-abnegation from the start. It tells him that to be strong, effective, brave, fruitful in noble deeds, he must serve rather than command, endure rather than attack, suffer rather than retaliate, believe rather than doubt. Powers ordained of God and running through the whole circle of legitimate authority, mould his will, direct his affections, demand his obedience at every step. He is never free from their pressure, and cannot without peril and loss ignore the obligations which they impose. He conquers by refusing to fight, and deals the heaviest blows by not striking at all. And as for his own highest interests, he best promotes them by promoting those that have the least obvious connection with his own immediate advancement. It is needless to linger on what this ideal has done for mankind as a whole, or for the glory and power of the individual. Its record is the record of the Son of man, its service for humanity, His service. It raises no question of "idle passivity on the one hand, and abundant labor on the other;" but simply how every soul can work most and work best for the ends God has set before it.

Such, briefly, is the witness of Christianity as to the best training and the best type of the individual man. It would be hard to imagine any more radical contradiction of them both than that offered by this other conception. Its fundamental postulate is that if man would be himself he must assert himself, that his own life when thrown into the scale is the sufficient counterpoise to all life beyond him, and that institutions are accidental rather than essential factors in his development. If he is to grow, it must be by the exercise of his rights rather than by the performance of his duties. To stand fast in his lot is to smother his energies. No assignment of vocation can be considered Providential that checks his ambition or limits the possibility of success. Thus the measure· of his desires becomes the measure of his capacities; and thus, too, character, from being a tranquil, duly proportioned resultant of healthy powers working for healthy ends, degenerates into a disorderly and feverish exponent of self-seeking and ill-regulated aspirations after things unattainable and perhaps utterly visionary. There is in this training the assumption that every man, whatever his station and surroundings, has in him the elements of some sort of greatness; and then it is assumed that, being thus endowed, every man who fails of advancement, must be an idler, or a groveller or a coward. With the estates and ranks of society ever turning on the wheel of change, with Senator-ships and Governorships, with Magistracies and Presi-dencies, and the vulgar power of sudden wealth equally open to all, that man is apt to be thought incurably weak who is satisfied with what he is and aims not to be something else. The star of destiny is believed to hang over the humblest, and it will be their own fault if they do not follow its leading until promotion is won, and with it the chances of assured fortune and fame. Children learn this faith with their alphabet, and too often begin life with an ambition whose restless craving only repeated failure and disappointment in after life can subdue.

It is quite likely that of English life this would be an overdrawn picture. I speak of a phase of character which Democratic Individualism is building up the other side of the Atlantic. And what I say has a meaning for you; for, unless I greatly mistake the signs of the hour here, American life is only the advanced guard of tendencies which are asserting themselves more and more alongside the more stable life, and in the midst of the venerable institutions of this ancient Realm.

(II) Let us now note the influence of Individualism on Morality. I shall grant at once, in discussing this point, nearly all that is claimed by those who are most sensitive to the dignity of the individual; namely, that it is his right to decide in the last resort in all matters of personal obligation; that he should never act against his conscience: and that to the full extent, that he is responsible for his conduct, must be his freedom and authority in determining for himself the conflicting moral interests which environ him. In this sense the language of the Apostle may not be qualified, "Whatsoever is not of faith is sin*." It will be granted, moreover, that it is the aim of all moral discipline to build up habits of conscience that will take the place of outward statutes and ordinances, and to substitute an inward character for an external law. These are all essential factors in the development of the individual: and the only question is, as to how they are to be brought into action—how they are to guide and to govern in all ultimate issues of personal duty. The right to do so is conceded, but the conditions under which the right is to be exercised require consideration.

Now Individualism in its relation to Morality is understood to mean an undue assertion of the right without a needful regard for the proper conditions of its use. Certainly, it will not do, it is neither wise

* Romans xiv. 23.

nor safe to trust the individual, as things now are, to settle absolutely for himself, and so to some extent for others all questions of duty, all claims of law, all demands made upon him by the authority of Church and State, or even of the Family and of general Society. He is yet a long way off from the intelligent and balanced mastery of self which would justify such a trust. Outward guides civil and ecclesiastical must still and for a long time to come stay his often feeble steps and light up the dim gropings of his moral reason. The end of the law is righteousness: but he is yet so remote from the end that the law cannot safely silence its thunders or veil its lightnings. Calvary has interpreted in fact and fulfilled in idea the meaning of Sinai: and yet Sinai still lifts its gloomy top behind every conscience not washed in the blood of the Lamb and "purged from dead works to serve the living God*." Great reliance, I need hardly say, is put upon education as the sufficient guarantee against any abuse of the individual's liberty of choice. The more advanced nations seem to be staking their hopes on it. Unfortunately they are not thinking of an education ethically as well as

* Heb. ix. 14.

intellectually complete—an education that builds up intelligence and morality on religion: but of an education that exhausts its mission as a gift or requirement of the State by qualifying the individual for secular functions:—*i.e.* to earn a living, to use the ballot discreetly, to handle, it may be, political dynamite without blowing up himself or others, to be conservative as against sudden revolutions that would endanger vested interests, to mind his own business when society does not call upon him to mind its business, and, generally, to be a considerate, safe, steady-going, patriotic citizen of the commonwealth of this world. It is a delusion and a snare to suppose that this sort of training can be an equivalent for the wider and deeper one that deals with the whole man, his will and conscience as well as his faculty of knowing that two and two make four, or of discerning what is safe, prudent, expedient, useful. Experience has shown us that the one is very far from implying or pledging the other, and that the State is neither willing nor able to make it do so. The policy of the State with us (in America) is the inevitable result of its attitude toward any recognized religion. It has determined, on the one hand, that religion is none of its business,

and, on the other, that education is its business. It
turns over, therefore, the one to voluntaryism to get
on as best it can, and holds the other in its grasp as
a creature of law. It does not encourage, far less
enforce an infidel training; nor does it concern itself
to prevent it.

What the effect is to be in the next, if not in the
present generation is no mystery to those who have
come to see either by inquiry or observation the
rising, widening tide of a faithless, godless secularism.
There is one nation, at least, that is already, especially
among its more thoughtful classes, beginning to understand that mere knowledge is not an unmixed
good, that Christless schools do create some suspicion
that all will not be safe for other generations and
that possibly the withes and bands of a secular state-
craft will not hold, in their proper orbit of liberty and
obedience, huge masses who have been taught to
know their power, without being taught to know
their responsibility to God for the right use of it.
Except God shall change the constitution of the world
and of humanity, a highly developed brain will not
offset a shrivelled conscience; nor will knowledge
take precedence of duty; nor will a secular education

prove a veritable sacrament to man even in the work of his temporal salvation. The education, then, now most widely accepted gives no promise that, for the present, the individual can be trusted, more than he has been, to act absolutely in and for himself as the supreme arbiter in the court of duty and conscience. The time has not come, as Individualism claims, for turning over to his keeping the outward law of morality, or subordinating to his will the institutions ordained of God and man to enforce and perpetuate it.

Again, neither the Christian standard nor the Christian type of morality is safe in the hands of Individualism. The standard refers to the degree in which in different times the recognized virtues are enjoined and practised; the type refers to the relative importance attached to particular virtues or particular groups of them*. Now Individualism cares chiefly for what magnifies the independence of the individual and only subordinately for the things that overshadow and control him. It may not be hostile to an exalted moral standard ideally considered, but its inclination will always be to dilute and lower it in practice.

* Lecky's "European Morals," Preface. Bampton Lectures for 1873, pages 5, 6.

The natural man when confronted by the severities of the moral law is instinctively tempted to keep within as narrow limits as possible his actual responsibility. He is never lacking for reasons why somebody else should obey and himself be excused. It is astonishing how under the clearest light the conscience will lapse into vagueness and flabbiness as an interpreter and enforcer of practical obligations. No amount of instruction or discipline can keep it fully abreast of its proper office. We see this constantly cropping out in its dealings with "sin which is the transgression of the law*." It is never the guilty thing to the eye of man that God declares it to be. It is a mistake, a weakness; it is caused by unfortunate limitations of faculty, or by an ignorant misapprehension of what the law demands: or it is an inherited fault running in the blood and so not deserving to be punished; it is any thing and every thing but that which excites Divine justice and calls down upon the offender merited penalty. On these and kindred grounds no moral standard, far less the Christian, is safe in the exclusive custody of the individual and apart from the sanctions which the eternal Lawgiver has planted behind the law, or from

* 1 St John iii. 4.

the visible ordinances that announce and emphasize
them. And then with regard to the type of morality,
only loose and disorderly dealing can be looked for
from Individualism. Countless influences are at
work to produce disintegrating fluctuations in the
current estimate of the virtues and vices of human
life. The processes by which the moral taste is
unsettled and often radically modified are subtle and
intangible, but not the less sure in their operation.
History tells us how, for reasons difficult to assign,
first the individual, and then companies of individuals,
and then society itself have inclined now to the heroic
and now to the amiable virtues; now to sins and
vices of the intellect and will, and now to those of
sensual appetite; and History tells us, too, how hard
it has been at all times to secure a hearty recognition
of qualities that immeasurably transcend either the
heroic or the amiable; and for the reason that they
are the gifts of the Holy Spirit, and as such can
abide in man only as he rises above himself and
becomes like God, and by this likeness a partaker of
the Divine life. Individualism, then, can be accounted neither the friend, nor the safe custodian of
an exalted natural, far less Christian morality.

(III) But from Individualism as it affects cha-

racter and morality, I turn to it as it affects the
Faith, Ordinances, Worship and Polity of the Church.
I may not do more than allude to the Ecclesiastical
System which has done so much to create the extreme form of it with which I am required to deal.
That Modern Popery by its despotic rule and un-
relenting intolerance is largely responsible for some
of the worst evils of Individualism, none but its own
disciples will deny. How and why it is so are
questions that my limits will forbid me to handle.
Partly as a result of the religious dissents, protests
and antipathies of the last three centuries, and partly
as a result of the social, political and speculative
tendencies associated with and respectively repre-
senting them in their kindred spheres, the Individualism of our time has already arrived at certain
conclusions within the province of Religion which
it announces not only with boldness, but with almost
impatient dogmatism. It speaks, indeed, on some
very vital issues as though, to the enlightened
thought of the day, the debate were already closed.
We are told, for example, by some Christian teachers as well as by many anti-Christian thinkers
that the individual is the master, and that all

organizations external to him of whatever name or
source are his servants; and further that, if they
are not willing to serve him and to be modified
according to his mandates, they have outlived their
time and are fit only to perish. It is declared to
be the teaching of experience, not less than of the
philosophy of History, that institutions are often
in their origin the creatures of great personalities,
and that it is the habit of mankind to cling to
and transmit them long after the impulse or emergency that gave them being has died out. At best,
it is claimed, that they are only the shifting "time
vestures" of the ideas, and aims, and forces of the
race. That they may have some connection with
a Divine plan in History, or that God's Providence,
as a power secretly directing and fashioning human
wills and judgments, may have something to do with
their origin and continuity is, with the advanced
doctrinaires of Individualism, an obsolete theory.
Thus resolved into issues of the unfolding consciousness of the individual, they have no life tenure save
that chartered by his will—no claim upon his obedience save that resting upon his voluntary consent.
Thus the only *vox Dei* that he is bound to respect

is the *vox populi*—or the utterance of any number of individuals greater or less, moving on the same plane and subject to the same conditions as himself.

For the present, I may not stop to inquire how this doctrine affects the framework of society or the foundations of civil government. Religiously and ecclesiastically considered, it is so radically false or so radically true, as, in either case, to swallow up all minor controversies. If it be true, then, as necessary corollaries from it, we must admit that, "as the web comes out of the spider, so creeds, ordinances and polities come forth from the inner life of man, and with a character in strict harmony with that inner life:" that the visible Church is only a gradual outgrowth from the spiritual needs and aspirations of the individual soul and hence without any divine and immutable principles in its structure; that truth has its ultimate basis in the moral instincts and its final criterion in the reason of the individual. But if this be true, then we are confronted with certain other deductions as momentous as they are inevitable. There is neither room nor ground for an objective, supernatural Revelation. Theology in substance, as well as in form, is a product of the human mind. God Himself, so far from being what Christianity declares, dwindles away into a vague and impotent reflection of the creatures whom He is supposed to govern. The Kingdom of Christ is no longer like its Author— the same in its organic being yesterday, to-day, and for ever; but lapses into the category of the perishable elements of History. The Faith once and for ever delivered shares the same fate; for truth grows with the growth of the human consciousness, and therefore no belief can be said to be final in the sense of being incapable of essential change both by addition and subtraction. Worship emptied of unchangeable verities, without a revealed and therefore a fixed object, without a revealed and therefore a fixed mode of access to its object, ceases to include the confession of a true faith and degenerates into a sentimental utterance of human needs and desires. It is no longer "We praise Thee, O God, we acknowledge Thee to be the Lord. All the earth doth worship Thee, the Father Everlasting;" but we are lonely and weak, empty and out of joint, perplexed and distressed with

> ....the burthen of the mystery
> Of all this unintelligible world;

and we would be comforted by pouring our cries into the ear of we know not what; but whatever it be, unless it have some help for us, it must be a heartless, headless phantom—all the worse for its inconceivable power and immensity. The Sacraments of Religion, so far from being anchored to the Rock of Ages and assuring us of God's gracious favor and goodness and of our oneness in Christ, are no more than arbitrary signs whose only power to affect us is derived from our superstitious veneration for material forms. Christian discipline, which prescribes and regulates the exercises of personal religion and brings the animal into subjection to the spiritual man, withers away into a conventional arrangement of human wisdom and convenience. And, finally, the Christian Priesthood instead of being constituted and commissioned of God—a veritably Divine ambassadorship from the Court of Heaven sinks into a function that has no higher origin than the instinct or necessity which leads all human societies to provide for an orderly subdivision of labor.

Nor are these all the consequences of this ultra individualistic tendency in Religion. For I have yet to mention the confusion and distrust which it creates in the sphere of Christian evidence. If we accept its premises, its conclusions in regard to the available proofs of Christianity are inevitable. The subjective method resting upon intuitions or the so-called necessary truths of consciousness is all that is left us. The whole mass of external evidence is surrendered at a blow, as having no solid ground of defence against the open assaults or the secret sapping and mining of modern criticism. If the intuitive convictions of the individual mind be the only ultimate criterion of truth; if every reader of the Holy Scriptures must find in himself the only sure evidence of their truth; if our faith has no firm props to lean upon outside the soul itself; no anchors to hold by save its own feelings: then it follows irresistibly that Christianity has no impregnable historic proof to support it, and that, thus, it ceases to be a historic religion and resolves itself into a mere exhalation from the " inner life" of man.

But it is clear that, if Christianity be dislodged from history and all testimony be barred out as useless and incompetent, the mind has no refuge against absolute unbelief except its own notions of truth: and truth, when cited to appear before this inward court, is forced to prove itself by itself and apart from its place and operation in history. Any argument based on external evidence is sneered at as empirical; any reference to historical data is rejected as irrelevant. Revelation is true not because it is authoritative, but authoritative only to the extent that it is seen to be true. Christ is accepted not because of His miracles, but in spite of them. What each man's consciousness does not verify is incapable of verification by any other witness. To this one witness we are tied up; and, this failing us, we drift helplessly out into the dark unknown.

I venture just here only these two comments. Individualism, while shutting us up to our instincts or intuitions, is obliged to admit that, at most, they are only half articulate even in the wisest and the best; and that for the great majority of mankind they are a mute presence in the soul—monitors that do not admonish—guides that do not see—witnesses that cannot be trusted—vague hints that one soul cannot communicate to another—secret visions that each must possess for himself in order to understand them and that vanish in the effort to describe or embody them. And next it seems a pity, that our

Lord could not have foreseen the lofty stage to be
reached by our Nineteenth century consciousness.
Had He done so, He would have been saved the
trouble of doing what He did to manifest and certify
His Divinity, of sending the Holy Ghost to guide
His people into the way of all truth, of preparing
through inspired men the Record of His life as a
precious heritage for the ages, and, lastly, of estab-
lishing and endowing His Church as the Keeper and
Witness of that Record.

· It is impossible to estimate the mischief wrought
by this tone of thought in the field of Christian
evidence. With a folly that would be ridiculous
were it not followed by such fatal consequences, and
alas! with the countenance of not a few in the very
home of the faithful, it complacently hands over to
the enemy the outer defences of the faith, which, in
their place, are as solid and tenable as the interior
ones of consciousness. It sunders what Christ Himself so joined together as to be incapable of
divorce—the light within and the light without
the soul, the moral reason and external testimony,
the intuitions of the spirit and the supernatural
facts of History which shape and voice them to

the eye and ear of our every day life of belief and duty.

(IV) But I pass on to other vicious fruits of an exaggerated Individualism. There is scarcely anything of more value in itself, or of more beneficent influence, than what are known as the Traditions of the race, assorted, compacted, unified by the lapse of time. There is no department of life exempt from their sway, or independent of their life giving currents. In them we see with the eyes, hear with the ears, work with the hands of the many sided past. Through them we live over again the thoughts and deeds, the agonies and triumphs, the burials and births of by-gone generations. They are, so to speak, the sacramental signs and seals by which History affirms and certifies the unity of the race amid all diversities of lot, and the mighty sweep of a providential purpose that goes on increasing with the ages, flashing out, here and there, like an unearthly flame in new enthusiasms of religion, new phases of knowledge and art, new advances of civilization. These Traditions are all memorable for their origin and growth, and often mysterious and almost sacred in their power to affect us.

Now if these Traditions have one enemy more formidable than another, it is that type of Individualism now under review. It has more interest in the future whose character it may help to shape, than in the past by which itself has already been largely shaped. Jealous of the authority of living institutions, it is still more jealous of Traditions deemed dead because the wills and minds that gave them being are dead. Setting itself up as the sufficient measure of whatever claims its assent, it regards with impatience all that transcends it, proves too large for it, laughs at its pride, exposes its weakness, prophesies the failure of its hopes, and strips its plans of the conceit of originality. Thus it finds a certain pleasure in clipping and paring away these honest, unshrinking reminders of its littleness in the eye of History. Whatever the cause, Individualism has a poor opinion of all transmitted, inherited wisdom, and so a very onesided and superficial one of the more silent, but really governing elements of progress. It is its habit to narrow the area and discount the strength of all forces not born of its own will, not nursed by its own thought, not plastic to its own wish. So far as it does so, it turns what is positive in the life of the individual into a negative as regards the greater life of humanity at large. Thus it not only breaks in upon the order of human growth, but blights and impoverishes the mind itself. Negations whether in the world of thought or the world of action starve, not feed us. All inspiring fervour, all living energy, all yearnings that open up to the soul even glimpses of a true greatness dread them as plants dread mildew, or human bodies the touch of palsy.

But further, as might be expected, Individualism has an affinity neither weak nor obscure with that most formidable of negations in these times— Agnostic materialism; or, if affinity be too strong a word—then a connection that renders it easy to pass from the one to the other. Somehow the laws of thought will have their revenge on those who forget or despise the inherent limitations of co-ordinate, fundamental truths. Excess breeds defect, extravagance poverty, too much liberty the destruction of liberty, too great pretensions of will fatalism, too much idealism in dealing with matter, the loss of spirit in matter. And so under the same law of reaction, as experience shows us every day, some minds disgusted at the religious contradictions and anarchies of the hour leap at a bound over the gulf that yawns between Protestant licence and Papal despotism; while others in the sphere of philosophical thought and even of social life, distracted and worn out by the evils consequent upon an extreme assertion of free will and a lawless use of reason, jump, with scarcely an intermediate pause, from the strongest, wildest doctrine of self-sufficiency and self-government to the doctrine which converts man into a passive, transitory link in a fatalistic chain, and so into the slave of outward circumstances, thereby wiping out at a blow the consciousness of freedom, the sense of sin, the dread of remorse, the horrors of shame, and with these the conviction that the individual soul could have been better or worse than it is. And what is this but Agnostic materialism pushed to its logical results on the ethical side of human life. But further, if it be true, as our ultra-Individualism affirms, that all knowable truth is evolved from, and conditioned by our personal consciousness, then it is certainly made less difficult to adopt the more radical proposition that consciousness itself is only an evolution from something lower than itself; and this readily paves the way for the theory that the highest life we know is only "a refined organization of dirt." I speak of a tendency, and I speak of it thus to show how needful it is that we should see it in all the gravity of its possible consequences.

(V) But turning from the more abstract phases of the subject, let us look at it, briefly, as it bears upon more obvious interests. And, under this head, I remark, first, that Individualism tends to an undue exaltation of the power of Public Opinion and to a corresponding depression of the power of authoritative and permanent Institutions. At least one effect of this on the individual is to narrow his range of thought, to relax his sense of duty, and to fetter his proper independence of will and action. It is curious to see how the individual, in the effort to assert himself as the foremost figure in modern life, has succeeded only in changing his masters, without sensibly abating the tyranny that exacts his obedience. While seeking to lift himself into supremacy over external organizations of every name, he has been building up another external power that threatens to rule him with a rod of iron. This new Autocrat—Public

Opinion is intolerant of appeals from its established verdicts, chastises the rebellious into submission, admits no responsibility for the wrongs it inflicts, drags down at a word the mighty from their seats, and with a nod enthrones its favorites chosen from the multitude, it may be, in moments of passion or caprice. It would be a just and generous master, and so a wonderful advance upon any previous form of power, if it could give any guarantee that only the best elements of popular life would enter into its composition. But alas! with the best it absorbs the worst. It must include all that lies at the base, as well as what rises to the top of the social fabric. It is at once the child and the slave of majorities; and the most charitable judgment on the tempers of popular majorities will not affirm that the power they wield is always that of the intelligence and virtue of the community. The Public Opinion with which I am most familiar, like the social and political system of which measurably it is at once the offspring and exponent, does not, as matter of fact, grow purer and wiser, as it grows older and stronger. It may be doubted whether it becomes more considerate and trustworthy as its authority expands, and its subjects multiply. As the supreme tribunal, it is so constituted as instinctively to level down, not up. If it does not make flattery of the masses, it certainly does make unquestioning obedience to the will of the multitude, the price of promotion and office. Too often a millstone is ready for the neck of every sort of leadership, every form of greatness that resolutely adheres to integrity and independence of personal convictions. As with the loftiest peaks of mountain ranges, so with the noblest spirits; when the thunder gust of popular passion sweeps the sky, they are the first and surest to be struck by its lightning. As in politics, so in religion. The pulpit, if not subordinated to, is dependent on the pews. Considerations of shelter and raiment and daily bread, cannot be excluded from the preacher's estimate of the freedom and independence which he may venture to exercise. So that under the absolute sovereignty of Opinion—a sovereignty built up in the main by modern Individualism, it has come true that the very theory of life that pets most and is most petted by the individual is the least tolerant of thoroughly independent individualities. Nor is this altogether confined to peoples most deeply imbued with the genius of democracy. For, if the testimony of one of your own profoundest thinkers can be trusted, a like tendency is not unknown here. He tells us that a sharply defined, resolutely out-speaking individuality is becoming too rare in English life; and that even eccentricities of thought and conduct may be worthily condoned, when regarded as protests against a monotonous uniformity which, if not, now and then, startled and interrupted will degenerate into a tame mediocrity*.

(VI) Again, Individualism has played its part of late in devising theories and originating movements for the reconstruction of society. No age has been so prolific of both as our own. Socialism, indeed, may be regarded as one of the leading characteristics of the century. Its first phase was Communistic. Of this the fundamental thesis was that all property is robbery. "Birth into the world entitles one to a living in it. Society in absorbing the individual becomes responsible for his support; while the individual, in being absorbed, becomes entitled to support." The second and now prevalent phase is

---

* The substance of a passage in John Stuart Mill's "Essay on Liberty."

just the opposite. So far from teaching that the individual is, or can be absorbed by society, it declares the individual to be the sole object for which society exists. It attempts to appropriate the social ethics of Christianity, and, at the same time, to eliminate all that is essentially distinctive of Christianity. It adopts the Christian view of the inherent greatness of the individual, while it rejects the Christian limitations of the idea; and so in behalf of the individual it wages war against the Providential and inevitable, as well as against the artificial, and therefore needless inequalities of society. No man, it tells us, is bound to acquiesce in a lot that deprives him of what some one else possesses, or to be resigned to any set of conditions that permanently interferes with what he believes to be his rightful happiness. He is sure of but one life; and it is foolish to ask him to sacrifice his comfort here for any possible compensation in any only possible *hereafter.* The individual is the foremost figure and the value of all things is to be guaged by what they do for him here and now. If social gradations and inequalities hinder his development, they are an impertinence and must perish. If capital refuses to share with him its profits on terms of whose equity he is to be the sole judge, it must be taught its dependence by dividing up its accumulations and making it give bonds for more liberal dealing in the future.

This type of Socialism, however lofty its exaltation of the individual, professes to repudiate violence and to care little for legislation. It appeals, with an enthusiasm worthy of Christian Apostles and Martyrs, to justice, philanthropy and brotherhood. But whatever its professions, its aim is that of an overdone individualism and its morality that of an atheistic travesty on the sentiment and purpose of the Gospel of Christ.

(VII) Finally, it remains for me to notice the influence of Individualism upon the Art impulse, the Art work of our time. The Art of this age is diversified and prolific beyond all precedent. There is no limit to its ambition, energy and industry. The earth spirit of the race never had so picturesque, so sensitive and so obedient an organ. It is genial, philanthropic, humanitarian. It is realistic, sensuous, imaginative. It has its dramatic, epic and lyric sides. It is tragic, serio-comic and comic. It is, moreover, justly distinguished for its learning and technical skill, as well as for a style of handling alike vivid, powerful and logically accordant with its own rules. And yet when we are through with our praise; nay, when we have uttered our Amen to the loftiest note of admiration struck by the most sympathetic criticism, there is still in it—the greatest masters themselves being the judges, an unfulfilled promise, an unsatisfied want, a sense of spiritual thinness and emptiness, a tacit confession of hopeless mediocrity in the midst of its wit and skill, its pomp and fascination, its abundance and versatility. Somehow while hovering near true greatness it just misses it and stumbles at the threshold of an assured immortality. Now if such be the fact, how has it come to be so? This question dominates all others in the realm of Art criticism to-day. It presses upon every cultivated and really thoughtful lover of beauty, and especially upon every Christian believer who sees in beauty one of God's revelations of Himself and in Art, as its chosen interpreter, one of the accepted auxiliaries of holiness. Some will say that the age itself is utilitarian and coarse, unideal and unaspiring; that Art expresses its spirit, and, in doing so, becomes like it. Some, again, will say that Art, like much of the culture of the time, has fallen too much under the sway of a view of life that takes the bloom and joy, as well as the seriousness and depth out of it; by dropping a blind over the eye of faith and forcing it to grind like some alien, captured Samson in the mill of "positive" knowledge; by smiting hope on the mouth because of the audacity of its visions; by robbing love of its true soul in the act of resolving it into a mere expansion of brute instinct or natural function; by treating every sign and expression of the marvellous as an enraged iconoclast would treat the images of a false worship; by flinging discredit, if not contempt on historic narratives which, if not penned with absolute accuracy of detail, yet picture to us with a loving admiration heroes and saints and martyrs of whom the world was not worthy. Others, again, will account for the fact by telling us that Art is without a creed, without a religion; that, infected by the spirit which has analysed and investigated and formulated God out of His own world, it has come to worship at a shrine turned into the grave of its own deity, and thrown away the key to the inner courts of the temple whose beauty it would explore; and having done so, is fated to move on a lower plane than the Art-life of classic Paganism, and to forfeit its hold on the purest ideals springing as they do, not from nature's order, nor yet from the mixed and clouded life of humanity—full as that life is of sweetness and light; but from the moral beauty and perfection of the Incarnate Godhead.

But however Art, ethically and religiously considered, may have turned its back on sources of inspiration which should be to it what the cloud by day and the pillar of fire by night were to the Israelites in the desert, this does not entirely account for its poverty along side of its admitted flexibility and productiveness. It may be that it paints and sculptures too much with an eye to good markets; it may be that it has no more thought of anything divine in what it portrays than have the craftsmen of Birmingham in the idols they cast for itinerant buyers on the banks of the Nile; it may be that much of it, like many living votaries of nature and culture, hangs on to the shows of things, "having no hope and without God in the world *." All this may be so, and yet there is one mischief making and, in an Art sense, demoralizing influence still

* Eph. ii. 12.

to be mentioned; and that is the influence of our exaggerated Nineteenth century Individualism. This may, at certain points, blend with, or spring out of the causes first named; and yet, in the mode of its operation and in the result it produces, it deserves to be treated as a distinct factor.

Now if it be, as is often claimed, the mission of Art to imitate nature it must take nature as it finds it, bound up with the laws and processes that govern the reproduction of its own forms. Nature is a perpetual new birth, and Art must be true not only to the things born, but to the laws which regulate their birth. Or, again, if it be the object of Art not merely to copy nature, but to create out of existing materials new forms that harmonize with nature, though not found in nature; then, to do its work well, it must adhere to the characteristic properties of the ideals which it seeks to embody. Still further, if this world had a maker and builder, then itself is the art-work of that maker and builder—the author and finisher of all ideal as well as actual beauty; and the best that the human mind can conceive or shape is no more than the dim and broken reflection of God's methods of building and fashioning in the world of sense.

Now if these premises be sound, it follows that Art completes its task only so far as it conforms to the divine patterns of things and to the divine laws after which those patterns were made. Now wherever God creates we trace a purpose and movement toward organic unity, a passing down from the general to the particular, from the type to the individual, a grouping of details around dominant centres. All things run out into a life larger than their own. Every thing is dependent on and finds its perfection in something else. Nowhere is the individual self-contained or self-sufficing. The landscape is made up of countless details each of little moment by itself and significant only in combination. The clouds are only dull vapour apart from the ether, the sun, and the underlying earth. The sea is blank, melancholy space until the light pierces its depths and gleams along its crests. The dawn is lovely only as it holds on its one wing the fading shadows of the night, and glows on the other with the radiance of the coming day; and the sunsets' glory is due as well to the segment of the heavens from which it recedes as to the curtained splendour into which it melts. So with grace, beauty, sublimity

4—2

everywhere. Apparently there is no particle of matter, no form of life, but abhors limitation to self as being first deformity, then death. Nature to the mind that reads it aright is always effecting the "transcendental" passage from itself to the thoughts mirrored in its visible forms, and so, too, is always escaping from its own bounded individuality into the greater life whose hidden harmonies it voices with a stammering tongue. We wonder not that Pythagoras rested in his doctrine of numbers or rhythmical order of the elements, and Plato in his scheme of ideas as the key to the mystery of creation. If both were no more than guesses, they, at least, were wise and ennobling guesses; and nothing has yet occurred in the march of the modern mind to prove that they did not bring their authors as near to the heart of nature's secret as the scientist of to-day is brought by his probes and crucibles. Those old Greeks interpreted God's works—the one by the law of proportion and the other according to the patterns of things in the heavens; and the now current theory of Evolution, so far as it is likely to have any abiding hold on reason must accept something akin to these interpretations, only adding the laws of continuity and uniformity of development, the end being potentially present in the beginning. In fact no philosophy of the universe has long attracted the human mind that has not sought and found in every individual part an idea, an energy, a life greater than itself could contain or measure.

Now it is the tendency of Individualism, as in religion, morals, social and political organization, so in art to ignore or reverse this law. Whether consciously or unconsciously it is inclined to contract, not expand the area of life for all things external to the individual, and so to sever, one by one, the bonds that connect the mind with the world of objective reality. Certainly this is its disposition toward all forms of truth not evolved out of the mind itself; and it is only natural, not to say inevitable, that it should feel in the same way toward all truth revealing itself in the forms of beauty, and, through them, appealing to our human sense of beauty, or to the art-instinct, the art-impulse. This disposition exhibits itself, as in other ways, so especially in a certain incredulous, morbidly analytical handling of all phases of nature, life and history that fall within the domain

of Art. The Art of the time has been a willing pupil
in the school of Individualism. It has caught its
temper and largely adopted its methods. Its attitude
is one of challenge, doubt, negation. It runs after
its own arbitrary *specialisms*, instead of surrendering
itself with a loving faith to the divinely constituted
unities of nature and humanity—unities which raise
individual persons and things above themselves and
bathe them in the effluence of a life deeper and
grander than their own. It paints human faces
as though they spoke for nothing but the single
personalities reflected in their lineaments. It paints
the great, the tragic, the passionate, the heroic, the
martyred life of history as though it had no hold
upon an ideal let down from the eternal world
and no purpose loftier than the circumstances that
immediately environed it. So with its sculpture
and too much of its poetry. It has been charged
with faintheartedness in dealing with the noblest
themes. Certainly, it seems to approach them
with a vague purpose and an unsteady hand. Its
firmest touches are confined to things which a hard
positivism has been willing to class among the facts
of which all can afford to feel sure. There is genius

enough, there is skill enough, there are industry and ambition enough to fill the century with an Art-greatness that would revive the memory of the household names of the race. It is not the lack of power that renders new Durers, Angelos, and Da Vincis improbable visitors among us; but the misuse, the misdirection of power both as to its processes and its aims. Our mediocrity is faith's revenge on our unbelief. It has been well said that "we are allowing science to browbeat us out of religion," and it is quite possible that we shall allow Individualism infected as it is, with the aggressive incredulity, if with no other trait of Science, to browbeat us out of Art. We know what happens to eloquence when it no longer believes what it says; we know what becomes of truth when it passes into the keeping of sophists; and we know, too, the doom of poets who are careless of what they sing, if only they sing sweetly. Briefly, our Art is cursed with poverty of spirit in the midst of its fine linen and sumptuous fare; and it is so because it believes, loves, adores as little as decency will allow, and doubts and rejects as much as it dares without utterly abandoning its mission. Acres of canvas and interminable files of sculpture rich in technical skill and intellectual vigor turned out, within the last ten years, and scattered among all Art loving peoples, might be cited to prove the charge.

But further, as the analytic, introspective, challenging, subjective training favored by Individualism hinders the search for spiritual truth, religious certitude; so likewise it stops the path into the realm of beauty. The anatomist's knife never yet brought him face to face with the life secret of the human body, nor can any mental analysis open up the life secret of beauty. It escapes the moment it is handled with a view to its dissection. "It is a revelation, not a mechanism, it is seen, not reasoned out." It is not built up part by part, but comes and goes as light through the heavens. So to speak, God argues for His own being at the bar of reason in three parallel, correlated, and yet distinct lines—the first and highest, the argument of duty or the moral law, the second the argument of design, the third the argument of beauty. Each in all its parts is true to its own line; each is perfect in its every individual manifestation; each evinces the unity of its source by the unity of its utterance and by the unity of impression which that utterance produces. As with duty and design in the constitution of persons and things, so with beauty. It is in all its varieties a repetition of the same thought, the same law, the same mind. It pervades every part, but lives only in the whole. Scientific analysis takes nature in detail, labels and puts away its facts on the shelf one by one; but its labor is only wind and folly when turned upon the pictures God paints on the eye. It may be, "that beauty is as much a phenomenon as oxygen or hydrogen; as good a fact as torpedoes or vivisection, typhoid or grenade shell or any other product of modern civilization;" but it is also an epiphany of mind to mind, and as such defies all inductive sifting and probing, grinding and weighing, and lifts itself out of the category of acids and gases.

Now so far as Art has contracted this analytic, curiosity-mongering, mystery-hating tone of the day, or has fallen into the hard, pounding method of science; so far as it disputes the presence of mind in beauty because it can construct no argument, frame no analysis to prove it; just so far it mars and shadows, not God's faculty to create, nor nature's power to manifest the beautiful; but itself and the work that embodies what is best in itself. The sovereign delight, the rapt ecstasy of an intuitive beholding of that which is nobler than the vision that reveals it withers and dies out with the collapse of the unreasoned, spontaneous confidence of reason and imagination in the truth of the vision itself; and with these perish the conditions of the highest art-power yet reached by human genius; and so goes down too the faith which sees the mercy of God in the rainbow and the glory of His love in the glory of the flower; while in their place rises that lame and wretched substitute born of our self exalting, materialistic culture, planed and squared into barren accuracy, seeing "in the eye no more than a crystalline lens and an exercise of nervous function : and in the sweetest smile no more than animal complacency lighted up by transitory sympathy."

Again, Individualism leavens Art with a spirit of *egoism.* As in other things, so in this, its favorite formula is the *me* equal to the *not me*, the individual poised against the universe. The world has had many sorts of *latria*, the latria of things, of idols, of mythical personalities; but it has been left to this generation to invent a new worship and with it a new name—

Autolatry. We need not wonder at this addition to the old shrines and divinities, when we remember what one of our current philosophies has done for this human self, by telling it that, if there be a God, His consciousness is not·only the same as man's; but finds its only authoritative expression in man's. Who shall set limits to the human ego, if this notion is to prevail? Now modern Art has not, we know, formally domiciled this idea; but it gives evidence of having been much influenced by it. Drawn into the well worn grooves of Individualism, it is doing much of its work on the maxim that, "nothing can come out of the sack but what is in the sack." In other words, every man is to himself the centre and circumference of rational life, and in listening to himself listens to the highest available authority.

I have already spoken of this temper as it affects character and the relations of the individual to external organizations. I have now to note its bearing on Art. It is almost an axiom of morals that to be unduly self conscious and to be great is impossible. As well say that the body can be hot and cold, moving and stationary at the same moment. What is true in morals is just as true in Art. All creative acts in the realm of beauty, as in that of letters, are unconscious acts. The mind goes out of and above itself, and, if it really create something, does so after an ideal too large to be shut up within its own "sack". The self conscious mind may have the power, but it cannot rise to the higher inspirations of genius; and for the reason that these inspirations break down the fences of personality, springing as they do out of sensibilities, passions, purposes which can become the property of the individual man only because they are first the property of all men, and so the gift of God to humanity. The Art-work, therefore, that revolves around the self of the worker loses its hold on the subtle energy and mysterious impulse of a constructive originality. It may copy well: it may combine with freshness and skill the materials within its reach: but it will do so after types and patterns thrown off, as sparks from the anvil, by the creative faculty of other minds swayed by a loftier spirit. Real originality is the product only of minds that gladly accept baptism into a life larger than their own—a life which, if it enter the soul at all, enters it, as light enters the sky or magnetism the body, without noise or friction.

It is therefore beyond the reach of the autolatrous mind. It has been rare in every age and it is so in our own. The world of Art to-day shows an astonishing amount of shrewd imitation, and of vigorous and ingenious use of existing material, and withal unsurpassed fulness and finish of elaboration: but its own masters confess with ill disguised disappointment its poverty of invention and original achievement.

Modern life is rich in novelty. It has thrown not only human interests, but human hopes and fears, joys and sorrows, in fact human passions and yearnings of every sort into new and commanding attitudes. Even the gross materialism of this generation has opened up fresh points of contact between matter and the power that moulds it, and has developed as never before the astonishing capabilities and latent energies of nature. Now all its achievements in this direction have their poetic side. To the soul of true insight the world has never been so full of the wonderful, the sublime, the graceful, as it is to-day. For the present, the ambitious mechanism of scientific progress may, to most minds, hold in abeyance "the music of the spheres," and grind up in the mill of law the finer tissues of sentiment. But the elect men of genius are bound to look beneath or above all this, and in their Art to catch the hidden pulsations of the Divine, beating evermore behind the passing pageants of our marvellous development of nature's powers. Strangely enough they are doing comparatively little in this way. The greatness of their work, as interpreters and fashioners of the sublime and beautiful, lags behind the greatness of muscular and mechanical energy. What they have done amounts to little more than tacking cheap fringes of Art on the flowing, kingly purple of physical progress. And were I to venture an explanation of the fact, I should find it in the proud, self-conscious, self-centred, self-sufficing Individualism of living Art. The "sack" has emptied itself, turned itself inside out, and found itself too small; and, instead of leaving its mouth open to receive the incoming riches, has practically sewed itself up at both ends.

Still further, in accounting for the leanness of Art, we cannot overlook, as one of the causes, the same *egoistic* temper toward the organic, continuous life of humanity. It has made not only the least of the past, but also the least of what is common to all men,

and the most of the present and of what is characteristic of some men, or of some classes and conditions
of men. It has courted popularity and patronage,
a quick market and prompt returns by speaking for
classes rather than for mankind, for the wrongs and
griefs, the ambitions and triumphs of schools of
thought, for reform movements, and special agitations
against this or that evil, rather than for the sub-
missions and protests, the pains and agonies of human
nature smarting under the ingrained inequalities and
diseases of the world's order. Art, whether as
painting, sculpture, or poetry may do all this, but not
as its foremost aim. These are the side eddies, not
the main current. But it is the weakness of the
egoist to mistake the less for the greater, the
particular for the universal, the fugitive for the
everlasting; and it is just this weakness that is
vitiating much of the Art of our time.

How different the line taken by the only masters
in the past whose names and whose works cannot die.
Dante spoke not only for "the ten silent centuries"
behind him; but for the heaving, shadowed, painful
life stretching further back—even to the Cross at
whose foot it cast the burden of its sin and sorrow.

So did the noblest ones who wrought in color and marble, in Art's noblest ages, when masters seemed to be sent of God, not called of men. Shakespeare left, among his creations, marvels of individual portraiture; but back of them all and higher than them all was human nature. Milton put himself in communion with the learning of all time, and, drinking in its spirit, reproduced what is essential in man, whether viewed in his relation to his fellowman and to outward nature, or in his relations to God's providence and government. Wordsworth, in a frame of feeling utterly subversive of self-exaltation and of specialism of every name, did the same thing, only in another way, when he said:

> "I have learned
> To look on nature, not as in the hour
> Of thoughtless youth: but hearing oftentimes
> The still, sad music of humanity,
> Nor harsh nor grating, though of ample power
> To chasten and subdue. And I have felt
> A presence that disturbs me with the joy
> Of elevated thoughts: a sense sublime
> Of something far more deeply interfused,
> Whose dwelling is the light of setting suns,
> And the round ocean and the living air

And the blue sky, and in the mind of man :
A motion and a spirit, that impels
All thinking things, all objects of all thought
And rolls through all things."

On the other hand, as an example of the self-spirit that dwarfs Art, I have only to cite one well known name in letters, though not a few others might be given who have exhibited the same temper only in a less degree. Criticism has done its task for Byron and nothing remains to be added. It would be difficult to find another instance of such wastage of power, or of so brittle a hold upon lasting influence by so commanding a nature. How he stirred and muddled the hearts of men is one of the traditions of the last generation. What he was and did found a voice not only in the morbid gloom and false fire of his verse, but in the supreme egotism that characterized his handling of all themes that fell within his range. His fame is what it is not merely because he took a soured and hateful view of life, or found in the deadly upas the favorite symbol of the world's order; nor yet because he accepted as a permanent experience what proved to be only a transient phase of passion engendered by the revolutionary phrenzy of his time : but still more because he put himself out of joint with nature and mankind ; and instead of finding in them a power to chasten and subdue, converted them into goads to his passions and blinds to his conscience.

This then is the sum of the matter, and, however imperfectly it may have been reasoned out, standeth sure that, (as has been often shown,) as Art cannot be truly great when the individual is shorn of the free play of his faculties : so neither can it be truly great when the individual pushes his liberty into license, his individuality into Individualism. Both conditions equally disturb the normal equilibrium between the inner life of man and the outward order and movement of the world in nature and in history. And if, in earlier ages, the best races and peoples had too much of the one tendency, it is quite certain that the best races and peoples, to-day, are menaced with, if they have not already accepted the dominion of the other.

SERMON II.

PSALM XII. 3, 4.

The Lord shall root out all deceitful lips, and the
tongue that speaketh proud things: which have
said, with our tongue will we prevail: we are they
that ought to speak: who is Lord over us?

IN the preceding Discourse it was my aim to trace
the growth of the individual: to show how he gradually emerged into the foremost figure in modern
life; to indicate the tendency in our time to develop
an eccentric, abnormal, extreme type of the individual; and to point out its exaggerations, abuses
and perils in the leading departments of thought and
action. Among the agencies that have contributed
to the healthy and lawful elevation of the individual,
it was claimed, that Christianity has been by far the
most prominent and influential; so much so, indeed,
that but for the general and profound sway secured

5—2

for its fundamental principles, the individual would be moving to-day on well nigh the same plane as that provided for him by the old pagan civilizations. He is where and what he is, aside from present faults and excesses, not in virtue of industrial and commercial advances, or of changes in society and civil government, or of the progress and diffusion of knowledge whether in the forms of literature or of science. These have all proved necessary auxiliaries in effecting his elevation; but the chief force—that which has leavened, combined and directed them all has been the Gospel and the Church of Christ. These alone could cause him to be esteemed and treated as made in the Divine image, and as a member of the universal brotherhood founded by the Incarnate Lord and afterward developed in history by the Spirit whom He sent. It was the light thrown upon man from the world invisible and eternal that opened up to him and to society at large his true position in the world that now is. Now if it be true, as has been claimed, that the progress of the race is dependent upon the progress of the individual; and, therefore, that the individual has still before him an indefinitely extended career of development; if it be true, too, that our age marks the beginning of an exaggerated estimate of the powers and capabilities of the individual; and if it be true, moreover, that as the Christian religion has been his chief guide and educator in the past, so it must continue to be in the future; then it follows that the teachers and representatives of Christianity are specially and eminently bound to deal with this deepest and knottiest problem of the time; and to discover and apply the remedy for existing or threatened disruptions and excesses growing out of the misuse or forgetfulness of the principles which, more than all else, have clothed the individual with his present dignities and prerogatives. In this regard the difficulty and urgency of the Church's work to-day are only less than those that confronted her, when she sent forth her master builders to lay the foundations on which her life was to repose through all the centuries to come. What then is the teaching required of us by this emergency? What is the attitude, the policy, the work now especially demanded of the Church?

There are two great divisions of Western Christendom whose antecedents and whose present temper partially, and, in some respects, totally disqualify them for dealing sucessfully with the evils of Individualism. Latin Christianity cannot touch them except as it opposes one extreme to another. In its dealing with the individual it repeats the error of the ancient pagan civilization. It cannot cure his excesses in the use of reason and liberty, because it denies what is lawful and necessary in both. It knows no way to remove cataract except by destroying the eye. It mutilates the patient in its attempt to cure him. It stirs up revolt in the act of demanding obedience. On the other hand, the unhistoric, disintegrating Sects of the day, so far from diminishing, aggravate the disease. Themselves the offspring of successive insurrections against and secessions from the Church's order, they beget the very things by which themselves were begotten. They are impotent to check a tendency, but for which themselves had never been born. The most impulsive and turbulent Individualism of the hour is only their own life pushed to its remotest consequences. They are moving so rapidly toward these consequences that they have lost control of their own drift; and so are powerless to arrest that of others somewhat in the advance. Now it is clear, in view of the position of these portions of Christendom and of an experience of their methods, that the needed teaching can come only from some other portion of it that in its organization, worship, faith and practical work evinces, on the one hand, its fidelity to the history; and, on the other, its adhesion to the organic structure of Christianity, and with these its equal regard for the authority of the whole Catholic Body, and for the rights and franchises of its every member. It must be conservative of all that God put into its keeping, the unchangeable verities, the unchangeable Sacraments, the unchangeable Commission, the unchangeable standard of personal godliness ; and, on the other side, it must be a loving, generous interpreter of the spirit of the age and a sympathetic advocate of progress in all that makes for the true welfare of humanity. Now so far as this great Anglican Communion, whose branches compass so many seas and continents, fills out these requirements, so far it can cope with the evils which have engaged our thought.

(I) To the question, then, what is the teaching demanded by these evils? I reply, first, and generally, that our Christianity must not only claim, but prove itself to be the only authoritative and complete exhibition of God's Revealed discipline for man; secondly and specially, that, with a wise adaptation of means to ends, it must urge with increased emphasis those truths of the Gospel and those aspects of the life and character of the individual and of Divinely sanctioned Institutions, which the present tendency is prone to disparage or to neglect. I shall ask attention only to the second of these duties of the hour.

To sober the temper, and moderate the claims of Individualism, we must strike at its core—its pride and self-sufficiency. As powers of disturbance and ruin these traits have never been absent from the world. But now they are not only specially active, but active in ways peculiar to this age. They threaten us from new points, and with new and more formidable weapons than ever before. It is not, then, new qualities or new aspects of man, but old ones in new shapes and in new fields of action that challenge our thought. Now these characteristics of living Individualism have sprung from divers sources—from amazing conquests in the material world—from an unparalleled quickening and development of the

intellect, and a corresponding extension of the area
of knowledge—from the vast ramifications of secular
empire as seen in the rapid growth of new states and
the peopling of new continents—from civil changes
that have diffused political power in some countries,
almost without limit—from alluring visions of progress in all forms and in all directions :—and finally,
from the general conviction which rolls like an
atmosphere around and through these times, that
where so much has been done nothing is hopeless or
impossible. We seem to hear it in the very air we
breathe—that it was well enough for less aggressive
and more ignorant generations to cultivate the self
distrust which properly attaches to infant races,
nationalities and civilizations ; but now in the ripe-
ness of the world, what temper more becoming than
one of unquestioning confidence and bold self-
reliance. When man could do little, it was right that
he should think and act accordingly ; but now that
the march of events has disclosed his power and
surrounded him with the grandest proofs of its
practically illimitable extent, it would be weakness
and folly if he did not bear himself as the worthy
peer his sublime opportunities. This is the temper

we have to meet—the Nineteenth century pride we have to humble, by holding up to its face the mirror of forgotten truths and forgotten facts. These truths and these facts are at hand. They are as manifest and indisputable as ever, and only require to be wielded with suitable courage to bring the haughty adversary to terms. In marshalling them for this purpose, experience and sound philosophy are alike at our service; while the wisdom, not of this world, speaking through the Gospel and the Church of Christ, is at hand to seal with a divine authority what history and enlightened reason declare.

But that the proud spirit now addressed might charge me with falling back on a dead tradition, I might cite the Holy Scriptures, and show how with one consent and with solemn earnestness they remind man in all his works and at whatever elevation, that his "sufficiency is of God," and that without Him he can do nothing. But why spend time in citing an authority before whose tribunal the adversary refuses to appear? Better, at once, to take him on his own ground, and deal with the modes of justifying his pride to which he habitually appeals.

(1) Now the first of these, as we have seen, is the

subjugation and control of nature. Man's dominion over the world has been wonderfully advanced, and yet, admitting all that can be claimed, how little has he gone beyond the alphabet in reading the vast outlying volume of the universe. He is still but the merest child in what he claims to know, as well as in what he has come to know. Natural Science, in its off hours, when released from the task of counting its triumphs, or of assailing received opinions is not ashamed still to hold up the few grains of sand on the sea-shore as the symbol of its knowledge. But turning from this thought, so familiar as to need only to be mentioned, I proceed to another not so familiar and far more humbling. Paradox though it may seem, it is nevertheless true, that the best measure of man's dependence on nature is his control over nature. The higher he enthrones himself in her domain, the greater his subjection. She extorts tribute from her conqueror at every step. She has her revenges for his victories and her reprisals for his intrusions into her mysteries. Haughty invader, she seems to say, in taming me to your service, yourself shall be tamed to the service of the paramount Lord of both; and for every secret you unveil, for every force you bind or loose, for every kingdom you explore, you shall wear some new badge of dependence, forge some fresh link in your chain; and all this until it shall become as true of your sovereignty, as it is of all sovereignties attainable by mortals, that this world has no thornless crown to give. Nature allows us to make dynamite out of the materials she supplies, but she tells us that its mighty force can be used only at the risk of the user. She has told us how water can be expanded to some 1600 times its normal volume; but in unchaining this tremendous power, she warns us that a very demon of ruin lurks in every throb of its energy, and is always on the alert for the careless hand, or the weak joints in the walls that imprison it to claim for its hidden altars whole hecatombs. The land is threaded with electric wires which act as though they were mere extensions of the nerve filaments of the human brain; but they serve indifferently the bad and the good, the devilish and the angelic in the life of man. The iron cleft from her sides goes into shot and shell, sabres and rifled cannon as well as into plough shares and pruning hooks; and so the silver and the gold dug from her bowels carry with them a curse as well as a blessing. Our chemistry has supplied us with marvellous stores of acids and gases, and with them not only increased ability to detect, but increased ability to conceal a thousand poisonous adulterations of our meats and drinks. Physiology reckons it among its noblest achievements to have discovered certain scientific devices for patching up and prolonging disordered constitutions, enabling what otherwise would have perished by quick decay to live on to a feeble maturity; and yet it is obliged to confess that, in doing so, it is debasing the stock and so impairing the ultimate prospects of the race. So, likewise, rapid locomotion, vast accumulations of capital, inventions that economize labor or relieve pain, while they are the accepted tests of material progress, hang upon the neck, sooner or later, of society and of the individual unlooked for burdens, unsuspected evils. Cheaper fabrics, cheaper iron, cheaper luxuries often mean cheaper lives, with a huge increase of stifled hearts and darkened souls. Our modern civilization, largely the fruit of this stupendous utilization of matter, with all its conveniences and comforts, has been but poorly studied, if it has not shown us the running sores it has opened, the wide wasting gangrene it has created. It is with no Manichæan antipathy to matter or any of its uses, that I note this side of a subject which, ordinarily, is the theme of unmixed eulogy.

There is no doubt that material progress has rendered important service to the moral interests of man; but the good it has done, though tenfold greater, should not hide the evils it has wrought also. And the moral of it is that this mixture of opposing tendencies, these shadows trooping after the sunlight, these pains dogging the pleasures, these penalties inflicting their revenges upon man for his growing power over nature remind, nay, compel him to remember that it is not in him to say, but in one who is the true Lord over him and outward nature what shall be the outcome of these triumphs. The more he governs the world, the more dependent he is upon that Being, who, as the Creator of all things, can alone rule the forces which he is permitted to evoke and conduct to beneficent ends the physical masteries which he is allowed to wield. That, then, which is man's glory, on the one side, brings out his dependence, on the other, and whatever call there may be for praise and adoration, there is none for boasting.

(2) Again, there is required of our Christian teaching a stronger and clearer message in regard to the value and uses of purely intellectual power and advancement. There is no pride that takes on loftier airs, or ventures more arrogant assumptions than the pride of intellect. Of its remarkable development in recent times, of the magnificent results of its exercise, of the part it has taken in the progress of the race in every age, and especially in our own there is no question; and the criticism now to be made will turn not upon the intellect, or upon what it has achieved, in themselves considered: but upon an almost idolatrous estimate of them when sundered from things on which it is God's will, as expressed in the constitution of man and society, that they shall depend for their true health and beneficence. Power of intellect, power of knowledge like any other power is good, bad, or indifferent according to the purpose it serves. It is the fault of Individualism that it is prone to glorify it with little regard to the aim that dominates it. This is no new vice. It asserted itself in the old Gnostic spirit: it appeared in the Scholasticism of later ages vaunting its ability to solve all mysteries by *a*

priori logic; but it crops out to-day more boldly than ever from a school of thinkers, who find in the growth of knowledge the chief, if not the only, impelling principle of human progress, and in the exercise of the intellect a surer and shorter way to the summit of truth—even God Himself, than by the uplifting energy of the moral affections. Now this fault can be met, not by walking up to it and smiting it in the face; but only by counter truths which demonstrate its weakness, if not its folly.

Now here the first counter truth is that, though this generation contains a larger number of intellectual men and women than any previous one: yet, as matter of fact, it has produced no men or women of intellect that, individually considered, are stronger than any in the past. It is idle to enter upon a comparison of names. It is, perhaps, enough to say that in looking back even among ages grouped around the childhood of the race, or among those commonly reckoned as eminently the ages of ignorance we find plenty of genius that our modern life has not been able to duplicate. The strength and glory of art, philosophy, letters, theology and even of war and statemanship seem to be behind us. We appeal, as by instinct, to the mental greatness of the by-gone centuries as our standard of mental power to-day. Besides this, there is the further consideration that the high average of intelligence among the mass has had its effect on the concentration of mental force in eminent individuals. As velocity absorbs power, so, it may be said, the wider the diffusion of intellectual activity the less likely will it be to retain commanding centres. The area of culture can be extended until it shall include every mind in the community; but it will be an area of mediocrity. The limits within which the intellectual property of each generation shall be confined would seem to have been fixed by some yet undiscovered law. The larger the number who are permitted to share in the estate, the more there are to resist the encroachments of great individual ownerships. Or to change the figure, given portions of the soil have each a certain aggregate of productive power. Each will grow a certain amount of timber, and it is for the owner to decide whether he will have a thousand trees of medium size, or a hundred of extraordinary dimensions. He can have number without bulk, or he can have bulk without number; but he cannot have both. The giant cedars of California with trunks twenty feet in diameter and lifting their tapering shafts three hundred feet into the air are intolerant of smaller growths about their roots. There seems to be something very like this in the growths from the intellectual soil. Certainly, the centuries that appear to have done most in the leading branches of thought and action are the ones that gathered up their energy into the fewest leaders. Whenever the door of discovery has opened out into new fields of conquest. and toward new empires, new civilizations, it has swung on very few hinges.

It would be well for this age that deems itself so self-sufficing and

"......Foremost in the files of time,"

to remember that it must accept the consequences of its choice—the reflection cast from its favorite ideal. Ambitious of universal education, resolved on the widest possible diffusion of knowledge, proud of its efforts to make every man, woman and child a stock-holder in the great intellectual corporation of the century, it must be content with its mediocrity and not repine because the first order of genius refuses to appear at its bidding. Fifty years ago, it was predicted that from the immense increase of printed matter and the vast accessions to the writing class there would be a corresponding augmentation of the imperishable contributions to literature. Where so many, it was said, are at work the greater will be the number who will achieve immortality. But somehow the law of averages has stept in to falsify the prediction. General excellence has been attained at the expense of extraordinary greatness. The lofty, solitary mountain peaks have been cut away to fill up the sunken places in the underlying plain. Whether it be that so many are satisfied with notoriety as a substitute for genuine fame, or whether it be a sharp competition for immediate gains, or whether it be the crudeness and superficiality attaching to hurried work—whatever the cause, there is an amazingly small proportion of the literary labor of the time that promises to be of permanent value, and still less that is likely to be ranked among the imperishable fruits of the highest order of intellect.

(3) Again, the pride of Individualism plumes itself on the rapid spread of empire, the founding of new states, the colonizing and development of

new regions of the globe. It claims these and all kindred movements as proofs of the intenser life which it has infused into our time; but the moral bearings of these movements are not free from doubt. They show the elasticity and vigour of the leading races—their ambition and capacity for expansion; they have relieved over crowded populations and have brought into a productive condition vast spaces of hitherto unoccupied territories—thus increasing enormously the commerce and industry of the world. But it may be questioned whether any new or higher moral elements have been evolved by all this restless stir and aggressive enterprise. Whatever the benefits arising from this order of things, thoughtful minds cannot but endeavour to rate them at their true worth and to caution the oversanguine against the false hopes which they are likely to excite. It does not follow that new states, because they are new, will be better than old ones, or that new continents with their cheap lands and vast areas will lessen the temptations, or curb the passions, or prevent the follies and vices that have always and everywhere beset human nature. Great colonizing movements only repeat with minor modifications the types of character whence they sprang. They who cross the seas change their skies, but not themselves. The stream of modern life may divide into a thousand branches—each cutting a new channel for itself and each flowing toward a terminus of its own; but it is not certain that any of them will rise higher than their original source.

New Babylons may be built as magnificent as the dreams of man can portray. New Tyres, new Corinths, new Alexandrias may be planted and by their growth swell the arteries of trade. But if they are to furnish little more than fresh specimens of accumulated wealth, concentrated power, commercial success; they will only repeat a story already too often told. Were such creations of modern enterprise multiplied by the hundred, it would be a vain hope that would look to them to provide any sure barriers against the return, in due time, of the corruption that sapped the strength, or of the moral uncertainty and spiritual despair that darkened as with Egyptian night the soul of the ancient Pagan life. Old Rome subdued worlds until she left herself almost without military occupation, sent out into remote regions her colonies by the thousand, created new centres of power among barbarous races and constructed vast systems of intercommunication between dependent provinces; and yet by them all she only delayed a little the final collapse.

(4) But closely associated with these activities and quite as stimulating to the self sufficiency of Individualism, has been the steadily increasing diffusion of political power, all the way from the qualified forms adopted by constitutional Monarchies, to the nearly absolute ones reached by Republics and Democracies. This too is an experiment that wise men watch with quite as much fear as hope. It is practically settled who shall be the depositaries of political power during, at least, the next generation; and now the tide of inquiry sweeps anxiously out toward the problem; given the power, what shall be the restraints and safeguards to prevent its abuse? given the power, will the multitude rise to the level of intelligent convictions and unselfish motives in its exercise? given the power, can the people be so trained by the education to which the State feels constrained to confine itself, as to induce them, not merely in every day affairs, but

in great and solemn emergencies decisive of the
rise or fall, the honour or shame of empire, to
interpret their true interests by an enlightened sense
of duty to God and to man? Or will the thing that
has been, come true again—when cheap lands fail
and migratory movements cease, and huge populations are shut up within impassable barriers, and
passions kindle and seethe under adverse fortune—
seedtime and harvest perhaps interrupting their
course—and men, finding that ballots are not bread,
and universal suffrage not the equivalent for universal comfort, shall rise; and, first trampling under
foot this coveted idol of our modern life, shall cast
themselves as pliant slaves at the feet of the strong
will that promises to win for them what all this
worship of the δῆμος has failed to confer?

Whatever may be our love of country and of
humanity; whatever our desire, nay our prayer, that
all these restless currents of political agitation,
steadily converging toward one point, may end in
nobler eras for the race, let it be said frankly, though
regretfully, that that man has studied history and
human nature to little purpose who can look into
the future without apprehension, or think himself

justified in speaking confidently of the certain peace, prosperity and glory in store for our posterities.

(II) I turn to another topic. As we have seen, Individualism has invaded the precincts, and, here and there, assailed the very citadel of Religion, as well in its Theology as in its Evidences. What, then is to be our attitude toward it? What are the counter-truths to be wielded against it in defence of this, the most sacred of all interests? While avoiding dogmatism, I would speak plainly on so grave a question. Surely there is little reserve or hesitation either in the pens or the tongues of the dashing liberalism of the day. Indeed, if the dogmatic, intolerant temper is to be found anywhere, it is no longer solely among the advocates, but rather among the assailants of the Catholic Faith that we are to look for it. This is no time for the heralds of Christ to so strain the precept—"speaking the truth in love*"—as to fall away into tameness of speech, or into certain easy, unchallenged platitudes of thought that have descended to us as part of the worn out religious coinage of a past age.

We are living in the midst of attempted modifications and readjustments of Christian Theology.

* Eph. iv. 15.

Much of our deepest and freshest thought is spending itself on these tasks. It is claimed that a conflict is upon us which renders these tasks imperative. I shall not here question the fitness or the urgency of this kind of work, though it is quite possible to overstate the demand, and, in doing so, to concede too much to it. Nor will I raise the kindred question whether, instead of attempting to mend the ancient deposit of God's truth, it would not be better to mend these times, curb their pride of speculation, heal their fractures, and bridge over the chasms which they have opened up between themselves and the old Creed of the Christian centuries. Be this as it may, there is one characteristic of these attempted re-adjustments of Theology that ought not to escape us. With few exceptions they all look one way. Some of them are intended to meet the special difficulties developed by the progress of physical science; some of them are carefully framed so as to afford the utmost rational satisfaction to man on grounds wide as the operation of his own reason; while others, again, seek to commend Christianity to general approval by enlarging upon the services that it renders to society and especially upon its vast contributions to the happiness of the individual. However they differ in other respects, they all agree openly or implicitly in this—that both the intrinsic and the relative importance of the verities of Revelation is to be determined by their power to move and to benefit human nature; and that every individual has the right to determine this for himself. The effect of this is, little by little, to limit the Gospel of Christ to humanitarian aims and philanthropic uses; and then to leave the individual to form his estimate of it by such aims and uses. The question with him quite naturally soon takes the shape that it really has taken in the popular mind already:—not what is the worth of truth in itself and as an emanation from the Infinite Mind—as an image and witness of the God who inhabiteth eternity; but what can it do for me? What is its immediate and practical use in bettering my condition here and now?

And so it turns out that God's word is precious only to the degree that the soul can, at any given time, taste its power and share its blessing. Only a little further on lies the thought that God is of use in His own world only as man is helped. Not the glory of God, therefore, but the welfare of

man becomes the chief end of Religion; and good
will to man, not piety to God the highest aspect
of the Church's life. This beyond doubt is the drift
of modern sentiment, the first and most striking fruit
of which is the "Ecce Homo" "enthusiasm of
humanity," now filtering through the pores of our
most popular Christian and secular literature, and
fast proving itself to be little else than another
phase of the far sweeping tendency toward the
undue exaltation of the individual. This "enthusiasm" has made itself equally at home, according
to circumstances, under the *Utilitarian* and the
Intuitional standards of morals—the one measuring
actions by their tendency to promote happiness—the
other finding in man himself the supreme tests of
truth, and both agreeing that the voice of God from
Sinai and from Calvary is to be subordinated to an
authority within ourselves which, practically, is not
the same in any two persons. Nor have we had to
wait long for some of its results. The glory of God and
the majesty of His law in the shadow; the promotion of happiness; the making all things in thought
and life plain, easy, and agreeable; the present
and secular well being of man; utility the guage

of moral values and spiritual powers; truth judged by each man's opinion of its use to himself; eternal justice thrust down from its seat, and false notions of mercy enthroned in its place; the stern sanctions of God's word regarded as fit only for infant or barbarous peoples, and altogether out of keeping with the gentle, amiable tone of our Nineteenth Century civilization; Christian dogmas discredited as so many impertinent restraints upon the free play of religious sentiment; and philanthropic benevolence, generally, the accepted substitute for the duties of Christian piety and the offices of Christian worship:—these without question, as they are among the evident characteristics of the age, so they are logically and sentimentally traceable to Individualism; whose extraordinary development in these times, be it observed, has been stimulated by both the Utilitarian and Intuitional subjectivism produced by the leading philosophical theories of the last generation. To return now to the statement made a moment since, the attempted modifications and re-adjustments of Theology which, of late, have attracted so much attention, seem, as a rule, to have been planned and executed in the interest of this phase of thought;

and, if not in open sympathy with it, they have certainly compromised themselves in the vain effort to bring it into harmony with the true foundations of Theology.

How then, is the danger from this quarter to be met? In the views now to be urged, the stand-point is a purely Theological one; and if the late reconstructions of Theology encounter the fatal objection to which I have alluded, what is the safe and real basis on which we are to build, or rather to defend what has already been built by the great masters of Sacred learning who, though dead, yet speak?

Theology must begin with God—His attributes, purposes, dispensations; or with man—his sin, weakness and wretchedness. Neither point of departure excludes all that may be developed from the other, and yet each imparts a characteristic tone to its own line of inquiry. As matter of fact, whenever Theology has begun with man, it has kept him at the front, has dealt less sternly with his guilt, taken milder views of his moral disabilities, given wider scope to his reasonings, greater authority to his intuitions, and generally conceded more than the facts would warrant to his powers and capabilities.

As a necessary result the subjective and human side
of truth has predominated; and, in one way or
another, the individual has emerged as the ruling
factor. And so we have been furnished with various
Theologies all insisting upon the common title of
Christian; and yet, in some cases, founded more on
what are called the necessary truths of the rational
consciousness than on the verities of Revelation; and
in others, while accepting the authority of Revelation
as a whole, interpreting and combining its contents
in an unhistoric and uncatholic spirit—each thinker
working for and by himself. Now of Theologies of
the former sort, whatever their local nativity or their
intellectual parentage, it is enough to say that they
have satisfied neither their authors nor their disciples; but, one by one, have yielded to the remorse-
less hammer of criticism, kindling, while they lived,
no enthusiasm of conviction or of conduct; but
ravelling out thread by thread and gradually wasting
away into impotence, are likely to be remembered in
the future as little more than the ambitious utter-
ances of transient schools of thought within the
domain of religious philosophy. Of Theologies of the
latter sort built upon Revelation, but by individual

judgments proceeding in ignorance or contempt of the Universal Church as the witness and interpreter, "the pillar and ground of the truth," it may suffice to say that their history is the history of the Sect movements which they helped to originate and are now helping to perpetuate. Now in radical contrast with both these kinds of Theology, stands the Theology that begins with God and lays its foundations on the rock of objective, revealed realities. As its matter is essentially the property and gift of Revelation, so its form will be determined by the testimony of the living, universal, continuous body— the Church, which Revelation sets forth and authenticates as its own highest and only sufficient witness and expounder. Thus both in the matter and the form authority will be the preponderating, though, in the form, not the exclusive element.

It is the characteristic quality and aim of Revelation not to reveal man to himself, but to reveal God to man; and so, by the knowledge of God, to enable man to know himself as he is. The surest way for man to discern his own condition and wants is by discerning what God in Christ has deemed it necessary to do for him. The only key to human nature is the Cross of the Son of God. Now the method of Theology must be the method of Revelation. It must interpret man by the scheme of Redemption : not the scheme of Redemption by man. It must erect itself upon and out of what has been revealed; not upon or out of man's instincts, or intuitions, or reasonings whether deductive or inductive.

And I pause here to say that, in the long run, the only Theology that can permanently command the assent, or preserve the faith of the English speaking race, whether in this Realm, or in other parts of the earth, is a Theology whose matter is made up of facts which, however they may harmonize with, are objective to and independent of the individual consciousness—a Theology resting on outward realities, not on man's notions; on what the living God has said of Himself and inclusively of man, not on what man has thought or felt, reasoned or conjectured about himself, and inferentially or inclusively of God :—a Theology, too, whose form, while recognizing every rightful prerogative of reason, will be cast in the mould and bear the superscription of Primitive Catholic tradition. Some races are habitually speculative, some habitually emotional,

some habitually imaginative ; but this race is habitually practical. Both by temperament and education
it insists upon having solid ground under its feet.
It has done so in Politics, in Morals, in Art, in
Philosophy, and eminently in Religion. It has often
been ridiculed, and even sneered at by neighbouring
peoples, because it preferred duty before glory as its
watchword, and common sense laws of belief on
the deepest problems of life before the misty and
often vapid abstractions of cloistered doctrinaires.
But, as well they might be, the laugh and the sneer
have been complacently forgotten amid the indisputable proofs of its enduring and symmetrical
greatness. And, in this connection, if I might
venture a special word to the younger now present, I
would remind them of this one thing—that as, in the
last generation, certain of our aspiring youths were
like to perish of hunger amid the husks of rationalism ; so, in this one, they are in greater peril of
having "the seeds of a wasting disease fostered by
the lukewarm damps and gilded vapors" of schools of
thought which, in the effort to develop all religion
from within, throw us back on spontaneous feelings
and beliefs; and teach us that Plato and St Paul,

Seneca and St John were alike sharers in an inspiration common to all great sayers and doers in the history of the race. And I exhort you to remember that so far as you allow any of these schools to influence your faith or your practice, just so far will you replace the rock of a true confession with the quicksands of individualistic speculations.

But if Theology should begin with God and accept as its primary ground the objective facts of Revelation; how are these facts to be dealt with? Having determined its *matter;* how shall we give it *form?* If it be true that the task is laid upon us of revising or readjusting Theology, so as to impart to it the flavor of living thought and to enable it to hold its own amid the conflicts and difficulties of the time, this question presses for an answer.

God's truth, the truth "which is the power of salvation to every one that believeth*" is in itself eternally alive because it shares the eternal life of its source. But to be alive and operative in human thought and life, it must, to some extent, at least, be so shaped as to have salient points of contact with the intellectual spirit of each successive generation.

* Rom. i. 16.

This can be done, in part, by recasting and newly adapting its general literature to the peculiar wants of the day. It can be done, in part, too, by so presenting it as to evince a just appreciation of all real progress in the several branches of knowledge, and notably in those claiming the most attention, the sciences of consciousness and the sciences of matter. Though in doing so, these two things must never be forgotten: (1) that no science of mind or of matter, of man or of nature can sit in judgment upon, or radically disturb any supernatural and revealed verity: (2) that the body of science so called and the body of ascertained truth are not identical; and consequently that Theology is not bound to drop out any portion of its traditional contents as human accretions at the demand of any or all lines of naturalistic inquiry, until it can be shown that their respective fields of investigation are exhausted and that there is no possibility of setting aside their present conclusions by a wider and deeper knowledge. But, further, it should be understood that Theology in meeting the requirements or in tutoring the temper of this age finds its chief task, not in reconciling with itself the admitted results of recent

knowledge whether relating to man or to nature;
but in holding the individual reason to its true office
in relation to things divine and eternal, and the
individual will within its proper limits as regards
the organic institutions ordained of God, or mediately
of Society for the education and discipline of man.

Now it is in this aspect and as bearing upon the
discharge of this task, that I desire to treat the *form*
which Theology is to assume in any proposed change
intended to adapt it to the "needs of the age." We
have seen what must be its matter; and, if this be
granted, we shall have gone a long way already
toward determining its tone and attitude, if not its
form. Now, in the interpretation and arrangement
of the revealed facts of Religion with a view to
bringing them into order and system, let it be
assumed that the Holy Scriptures have been rendered with grammatical accuracy, and that every
resource of contexual comparison and historical illustration has been applied. Still, as experience tells us,
after all this has been done, there is wide room for
diversity of opinions and conclusions. To what rule
or standard, then, can we appeal in the effort to
bring unity out of this diversity? By what authority

shall Theology be governed in the work of formu-
lating and adjusting the truths that make up its
matter ? I reply the Analogy or "Proportion of faith*"
as latent or implied in all Scripture, as specifically
referred to by an inspired Apostle, and as authorita-
tively developed by the Catholic Church.

Will it be said that this is a vaguely defined, loosely
jointed rule under which any and all religious thinkers
may build ? I answer that it has not proved so in the
past. The successive schools of divinity, during the
last fourteen hundred years, have aimed to harmonize
with it their respective peculiarities, or to correct
violations of it. It stands for the general symmetry
and unity of the whole body of Christian doctrine,
and for the right relation of every part of it to the
whole. It began with a body of truth possessed of
the attributes of unity, universality and perpetuity,
and rests upon the fact that the Church has never
been without such a body of truth. From the beginning of Christianity, it has been a recognized
and influential factor in Theology. In the nature of
the case it could not have been otherwise. "The
origin and first establishment of Christianity were by
the preaching of living men who said they were com-

* Rom. xii. 6.

missioned to proclaim it. There is a vague and unreasoning notion that Christianity was taken from the New Testament. The notion is historically untrue, Christianity was widely extended through the civilized world before the New Testament was written; and its several books were successively addressed to various bodies of Christian believers—to bodies that is who already possessed the faith of Christ in its integrity. When, indeed, God ceased to inspire persons to write these books, and when they were all collected together in what we call the New Testament, the existing faith of the Church*, derived from oral teaching was tested by comparison with this Inspired Record. And it henceforth became the standing law of the Church that nothing should be received as necessary to salvation which could not stand that test. But still though thus tested (every article being proved by the New Testament), Christianity is not taken from it; for it existed before it. What then was the Christianity that was thus established? Have we any record of it as it existed before the New Testament became the sole authoritative standard? I answer, we have. The Creeds of the Christian Church are the record of it. That is

* Romans xii. 6.   2 Timothy i. 13.   2 Timothy ii. 2.

precisely what they purport to be; not documents taken from the New Testament, but documents transmitting to us the Faith as it was held from the beginning; the Faith as it was preached by inspired men, before the inspired men put forth any writings; the Faith once for all delivered to the saints. Accordingly you will find that our Church in her VIIIth Article does not ground the affirmation that the creeds ought to be "thoroughly received and believed" on the fact that they were taken out of the New Testament (which they were not); but on the fact that, they may be proved by most certain *warrants of Holy Scripture**".

All essential truths, then, were as matter of history, gathered up into "the form of sound words" and were the things (as St Paul wrote to Timothy) "that thou hast heard of me among many witnesses: the same commit thou to faithful men who shall be able to teach others also." In that "form of sound words"—the product of Inspired wisdom, nothing was in excess, nothing in defect, nothing omitted essential to salvation or needful to express the mind of Scripture when Scrip-

* From a Sermon by Rev. F. B. Woodward, 1861. (Rivingtons.)

ture should appear in its completed form. That a body of truth thus framed and certified would be of the greatest service in all ages cannot be doubted. It was, certainly, so regarded by all the early Fathers and was constantly appealed to by the Primitive Church. The Anglican Communion throughout the world is what it is, because its Reformation was inspired and guided by an intelligent and steadfast obedience to this standard*. There has of late been much disputing as to the rival claims of the Deductive and Inductive methods in Religious inquiry. I have only to remark in this connection that the rule of interpretation and arrangement based on the *Analogia Fidei*, combines both methods and in the only way that it can be done with a due regard for their mutual limitations. It proceeds deductively in that it accepts the principles of saving truth as already established and formulated; and inductively in that it proves the Divine authority for these principles by collating the particular facts and teachings of Scripture on which they rest. The absolute validity of the deduction is assured because it was

* This subject is more widely treated in (Appendix C.) my "Conciones ad Clerum." (T. Whittaker, N. Y. 1880.)

the work, in great part, of Inspired men. The
absolute validity of the induction can be assured
only by the perfect discharge of the function which
it involves. The former is secure and cannot change;
the latter must always vary in force according to the
thoroughness with which it is done. The former
gives us the sacred deposit the same yesterday, to-
day, and forever; the latter gives us the proof, one
sided or all sided, partial or exhaustive, just as
successive inquirers perform their task. Neither
method can stand alone in any Theology that means,
on the one hand, to be at unity with the testimony
of the Catholic Church, and, on the other, to approve
itself at the bar of living thought. And yet in
defiance of this fact, the modern spirit would turn
over the whole field to the exclusive keeping of
Induction. It tells us that there is but one road to
truth whether in Theology or elsewhere. It demands
that we shall first ascertain the particulars of God's
Word, and then evolve from the particulars the
general principles of Theology—each inquirer working independently and accepting no helps, bowing to
no authority, yielding to no guidance that may
trammel the liberty of individual judgment. Now in

resisting this demand we are in the best of company and backed by a catena of authorities that includes the most illustrious 'names in the history of Sacred learning. It is opposed to the *consensus* of the Church universal, to the practice of Patristic antiquity, to the witness and work of the undisputed Œcumenical Councils, to the use of the Apostles, and finally to the method of our Lord Himself as the Supreme Prophet of the ages.

The Analogy of Faith, then, and the method based upon and regulated by it, cannot lightly be put aside by the new learning acting in the interest of Individualism. No possible increase of knowledge, however drawn from the various fields of investigation, can displace a principle which, from the beginning, has been immoveably rooted in the mind and practice of the Church of God. I have aimed to set forth the only safe rule by which Theology can be governed in any possible re-arrangement of its contents with a view either to a better adaptation of itself to the altered conditions of the times, or to erecting new safeguards of the Faith against the weakening dilutions and alien mixtures of individualistic speculations.

But as Theology is concerned not only with the

Faith as a system of truth, but with the Faith as a historic fact, it must be prepared to defend and prove the historic origin and development of the Faith, as well as to determine the method by which it is to be exhibited in the coherent unity of its parts. We have seen that it is one of the characteristic tendencies of Individualism in Religion to disparage the historic evidences of Christianity. It regards Christianity as an affair of sentiment, as consisting of ideas and forces capable of wearing any number of liveries, as purest and most real when severed from all positive historical relations, as finding its best and only needed evidence in the answer it gives to the wants and wishes of human nature, and generally in its moral suitability to the present condition of mankind. Show me, it says, that I need it, and you are done with the proof. It is a weariness and an impertinence to be pressing this or that outward credential, when every man's own consciousness is the only complete and satisfactory evidence*. So long as it maintains a solid footing in history, it is felt to be impossible to resolve it into a sentiment or an idea, and so to constitute every individual mind the final

* See Note 2.

arbiter of its value or its necessity. Therefore, to push it out of history, to disrupt and cut away its hold on history, to depreciate or deny the proof which history adduces is the one issue on which nearly all the forms of recent doubt have converged. It is, then, a foremost duty of the Theology of the time to insist upon a due respect for every kind of historic testimony, and so to exhibit every kind of it as to compel such respect. The great controversy has run through all intervening cycles and brought us back to the stand-point of the great writers on the Evidences, who, a century ago, drove from the field in utter rout and confusion the Atheistic and Deistic assailants of the Faith. Doubtless it was because they labored the subject so constantly and so profoundly, that the present generation of Christian scholars have so much overlooked it. But the time has come, when we must imitate the diligence, and do something more than reproduce the learning and logic of our fathers. From the beginning, in all the crises of doubt, the Church has urged, side by side, and, with a deep sense of their reciprocal help, both the philosophical and the evidential lines of conviction—the one dealing with the moral adaptations of

Christianity as the remedy for the sin and wretched-ness of man—the other with the argument based on the specific and incontestable facts of history. Both together make up the scheme of proof by which the Author and Finisher of the Faith intended to vindi-cate, through all time, the reality of His message, the power of His Cross.

Religion lifted above or thrust out of history may be a captivating vision for idealists and disciples of the pure reason and votaries of overdone Indi-vidualism; but it is not Christianity; and it is a wretched abuse of words to call it so. The Apostles, and first preachers of the Gospel showed man to himself as he never saw himself before—his diseases, his sorrows, his guilt, his utter helplessness; and then set before him the Cross as the only power that could pardon, heal, and comfort him. They argued out the adaptations to their final limit. And yet with equal constancy and fervor, they affirmed, "That which we have heard and seen with our eyes, and our hands have handled of the Word of Life, declare we unto you. Ye men of Israel, hear these words; Jesus of Nazareth, a man approved of God among you by miracles and wonders and signs which

God did by Him in the midst of you, as ye your-selves also know; Him ye have taken and by wicked hands have crucified and slain; whom God hath raised up, having loosed the pains of death *," Indeed, as has been well said, "whatever may be the case with other religions, the Gospel certainly never made its way by first recommending itself to the conscious wants and wishes of mankind. It seemed, on the contrary, to contradict all man's expectations, and to outrage all his cherished feelings, and to cross all his strongest desires." It was "to the Jews a stumblingblock and to the Greeks foolishness†." What was true at the start is true now. There are to-day, and there always will be the same antipathy, the same distrust, the same aversion, the same denial. Man will hate the light which uncovers, rebukes, punishes him long before he will love the light which illumines, warms, guides and blesses him. No man can have any real sympathy with the Gospel until he believes and acts upon it, and so brings his heart under its regenerating power. In fact, if he turn from its evidences on the plea that they have nothing to

---

* Acts ii. 22, 23.   † 1 Corin. i. 23.

do with his spiritual nature, or with spiritual truth appealing to that nature, he will turn with stronger aversion from the truth itself when it seeks to grasp his sleeping, benighted soul. Let us understand at once and put aside all deception in the matter, that when the natural man says that he wants no other proof of the claims of Christianity than its felt adaptation to his wants—its power to purify and uplift his affections, he is, as a rule, simply repeating the shibboleth of the sentimental idealistic school; or he is leaving out of the estimate of himself the one deepest, darkest fact of his being—the sin of his soul, the guilt of his life; and with that leaving out of his estimate of God the will and the power to punish interlocked with the will and power to forgive; and in either case he is conceiving of Christianity as something else, something less and lower than it is. He may take spontaneously to his own theory of Christianity; but not to the Christianity that finds its voice in the Cross and the corner stone of its evidence in the empty grave of the Son of God.

(III) But if we are to offer an effective opposition to the extravagant claims of Individualism we

must go deeper than any of these lines of inquiry
has carried us. Those claims have their ultimate
ground in the most profound and abstract speculations which the human mind has dared attempt.
So far removed, indeed, are these speculations from
the ordinary processes of thought that we wonder
how they can influence practical life at all. And yet
history tells us how the speculative abstractions of
one age are often translated into the popular thinking
of another, and specifically how the literature, ethics
and politics of any given generation are influenced by
the modes in which its predecessor may have handled
those final problems of thought and being that the
human mind seems to be as powerless to let alone,
as it is powerless to solve. The subject now before
us furnishes a striking example of this.

The favourite thesis of Individualism—man the
measure of all things—the human mind the ultimate
criterion of all truth, is almost equally the product of
the two rival philosophies which, however they may
continue to be discussed in our day, were worked out
in the last generation. The principle in itself, as we
have seen, is a revolt, in greater or less degree, against
all authority, not only in religion and morals, but

inferentially in all external organizations whatsoever. Some may think the principle sufficiently accounted for by referring it to the innate pride and ambition of the human intellect; while others, duly allowing for the influence of these qualities, will not fail to discover how closely all that is now specially characteristic of it is connected with the best known philosophical systems of our time. The influence of this connection may not be traced in detail. The most general statement will suffice.

If it be true, as the one philosophy claims, that we can know nothing beyond the things that appear, that all attainable knowledge is limited to a generalized experience, that causes, substances, things as they are in themselves cannot be grasped by us, that the absolute and the infinite are unknowable because unthinkable, that rational thought is possible only within the limits of the finite and relative:—if this be true, then it is quite reasonable that reason should infer that itself is the adequate measure and final criterion of truth. If, as you are bound to do by the fundamental principle of this philosophy, you subtract from the domain of knowledge God, spirit, immortality, and with these the Supernatural in every form; if you insist upon demonstration as the only authority, and accept science as the only revelation, nature's laws as the only providence; if you destroy Christianity and the whole world of thought and life which it implies by destroying the possibility of its proof; if, in other words, you so enlarge the compass of Materialism as to make it commensurate in the sphere of knowledge with the all in all of the Universe; then assuredly the human mind, as the organ of knowledge, puts forth no very great pretension in assuming to be the measure of all. The sovreignty obtained by thus dwarfing the empire over which it extends may be a real one; but it is not especially flattering to the dignity of human nature. While it helps to exalt Individualism, it narrows and degrades the individual.

If, on the other hand, it be true—as the opposing philosophy claims—that the absolute and infinite are knowable, that we can know things as they are, that we can pierce down to the underlying and essential reality, that the human consciousness contains in itself premises larger than itself and from which may be deduced rational conceptions of an infinite and absolute existence and of the laws and purposes by which such an existence is swayed; if it be true that man can furnish not only the materials out of which, but also the method by which, God can be rationally or metaphysically constructed, then it follows likewise that the individual may claim to find in himself the ultimate ground and measure of truth. If he is, in any form or relation, able to grasp the whole, then he may claim at once the power and the right to exercise his critical judgment on the parts. If he can compress Deity within the limits of his own consciousness, then he may do the same with all the operations of Deity. And if he may do the latter, then he may affirm, for example, either that a revelation is superfluous; or that, if given, its contents can be authoritative only so far as they approve themselves to his judgment.

To a mind that has thus learned to conceive of itself as endowed with faculties of knowledge practically unlimited in their scope, it will be no answer to its demand to say, that, though in the nature of the case all true revelation of the Divine must be rational because emanating from the Divine reason; yet that only what is *explicitly* rational is the proper object of human reason; while what is rational only in a latent and *implicit* sense is equally the object of faith. Tutored in the school now under consideration, such a mind will reply there is no validity in the distinction thus drawn. For if the difference between the reason of God and the reason of man be one of degree only, not one of kind—one of quantity, not one of quality: (as is affirmed by the absolute philosophy), then no limit can be fixed beyond which human reason may not pass in approximating itself to the Divine reason. Expansion and progress are the law of our rational life. What could not be fathomed yesterday may be to-day, or somewhere in the near or distant future. What this or that individual reason cannot comprehend, because yet confined to a lower plane of thought; some other individual reason may comprehend, because it has been widened out and lifted up by larger culture. Both theories of knowledge, then, not only can be, but have been so interpreted and applied as to furnish the philosophical ground of the root-principle of Individualism. The one establishes the supremacy of the individual mind by eliminating God and tying

up man to the things that appear; the other does
the same, on the intellectual side, by humanizing
God; and, on the ethical and spiritual side, by
deifying man.

Now we cannot handle this ground-idea of Individualism without being reminded that there is
nothing new under the sun, and that the thing that
hath been is the thing that shall be. Protagoras,
the Greek sophist, held the same notion. He advo-
cated it with an acuteness and cogency of reasoning
surpassed by none of its modern converts *. And he
made such free use of it, moreover, in morals as well
as metaphysics, as to compel both Plato and Aristotle
to honor him with elaborate refutations and so to
give him his only claim to immortality. This notion
re-appeared, as it could not fail to do, in many of the
arguments against Christianity by the early Pagan
rationalists. It cropt out again in the scholastic
scepticism of Abelard and his disciples: and the
part it is playing in the sphere of modern doubt
is only what might have been expected alike from
the history of thought and the innate tendencies
of the human mind. Such being the facts, the

* See Note 3.

question thrust upon us is, how are we to deal with Individualism as developed from this root?

As christian teachers and believers we may expose, and denounce the perilous consequences of this or that theory of knowledge : but we shall lapse into culpable folly, if we decry any and all efforts of reason to convince itself of the reality of whatever claims its assent or offers itself to the larger vision of faith. If it may be said of anything, it may be said of the reasoned speculations of the mind, that the evil that is in them is only "good in the making." As the times now are, intellectually considered, we must plead at the bar of reason, or surrender our heritage to some possible future vindication. We who are commissioned to speak for the Supreme Reason, as operative in the scheme of Christian Redemption and manifested in the Incarnate Word, cannot consistently or safely scout reason at any lower stage of its activity. The duty, then, presses upon us with a gravity and urgency which no tongue can exaggerate, to ponder deeply and wisely the plea we have to offer.

Now it seems to me that the first requirement laid upon us is to move with careful discrimination in dealing with the now dominant systems of metaphysical inquiry which, as has been seen, are not more hostile to one another, than they are, in some of their final results, hostile to the sacred interests that we are set to defend. Neither of them can we altogether accept, or altogether reject. Full of light and power as is the logic of Sir William Hamilton and Dean Mansel, we cannot accept it as final or complete. For, though, as presented by the latter, it was intended to protect the foundations of the Faith by an impassable wall, it was found, after critical examination, to justify inferences of which one of the most subtle of living thinkers has made telling use in building up the most compact and comprehensive system of scepticism known to this century. On the other hand, we cannot cast it aside as powerless or worthless: indeed, we cannot lose our hold upon it as a valuable auxiliary in certain stages of the Christian argument, because of the luminous precision with which it has traced the limits of all thinking that admits its amenability to the accepted laws of thought and with these the contradictions and difficulties from which philosophy, considered as reasoned truth, can never escape. So, again, we can neither accept nor reject, as a whole, the opposing schemes of

speculation that aim to bridge the chasm between
the relative and the absolute. We cannot accept
any of them, because, if they prove any thing, they
prove too much : and still more, because of practical
consequences, against the peril and extravagance
of which, both recent history and present experience
alike warn us. How else than with a feeling of
distrust can we regard, as well the premises, as
the processes and conclusions, of a philosophy
whose masters undertake to "re-think the thought
of creation," or to engage in *a priori* reconstructions
on moral grounds of the Word of God, or to find in
their own intuitions translated into metaphysical for-
mulas the only complete and authoritative revelation,
or to merge the Deity in the order of the universe
and to cancel personal responsibility by a pantheistic
absorption of the individual will? On the other hand,
we cannot entirely reject this theory of knowledge
without, so far as reason is involved, forfeiting our
hold upon the Infinite and the hold of the Infinite
upon us; and so cutting loose Religion itself from
its own anchorage. Thus it comes true here, as it
does within the circle of Christian inquiry, that
we must balance, as best we can, the teachings of

mutually repellant methods of thought and, in any event, maintain principles whose contradictions we can neither evade nor reconcile.

If the correctness of what has been said shall be granted, we are prepared to advance a step further in combating the philosophical basis of Individualism. Speaking generally, we are, as against materialistic positivism to assert a qualified moral and spiritual, if not intellectual, knowableness of the Infinite, and, as against the absolute philosophy, to maintain that man cannot comprehend, in the sense of reasoning out or rationally explaining, much that he is able to apprehend, in the sense of seeing and receiving, as the less accepts from the greater, as the part derives upon itself the life and virtue of the whole, as the member profits by the light that belongs to the whole body. Man's capacity to receive truth outruns his capacity to formulate it. He is able to know more than he is able to prove. His responsibility both moral and mental in opinion and belief, as well as in conduct, is measured neither by his logic nor by his metaphysics. It may be true that he has in him instincts, aspirations, thoughts that impel him to the endeavour to transcend his own individual consciousness—to

find or to realize himself in that which lies beyond
and seems to limit him: it may be true that along-
side of these or included in them there is a latent
sense of the absolute unity of thought and being,
subject and object, or of that absolute consciousness
on which all finite knowledge and existence rest: yet
neither that impulse, nor that endeavour, nor the
consummation of both, nor that latent sense of the
universal and absolute, nor the feeling of dependence
on them as the ground of all human personality, nor
even the sense of moral obligation implying both an
outward, unchangeable law and an eternal lawgiver—
none, nor all of these, however they may establish
the necessity of Religion and go to form the religious
faculty in man, entitle him to regard himself as the
final arbiter and judge of what God as the Infinite
and Absolute may have seen fit to reveal to him. For,
I repeat, his power to receive and act upon what is
offered him by external authority has a vastly wider
reach than his power to criticise what is so offered.
If then we concede to philosophy all it claims as the
result of its endeavor to lengthen out the sounding
line of the human mind, there will always remain
in the ocean to be fathomed depths which it cannot

measure. And, further, if this be so, then the human mind must seek the ultimate criterion of truth, the final basis of certitude, not only in itself, but as well and equally outside itself, *i.e.*, in a voice, in a word, a testimony, a Revelation the authority of which rests not more upon a reasoned assent to its contents, than upon the collateral, external credentials which attest to reason the divinity of its source.

It may be true that "whatever is absolutely inscrutable to reason cannot be made known to faith," and this because whatever is absolutely unintelligible and in this sense beyond reason is simply the negation of reason : but it is also true that there may be, nay that there is much within the province of reason, taken in its largest sense, that the present disordered moral state of human nature renders human reason incompetent to do more than humbly accept, without other challenge or criticism, than that given to the evidences which certify the supernatural origin of the message by which it is conveyed. Reason has its rights—sacred and inalienable rights. Let it exercise them to the furthest lawful limits. Let it claim all the light which a reverent and thoughtful investigation can throw upon the contents of Revelation.

Let it put forth its utmost endeavour to verify them, to disengage them from what is accidental, to develop their organic unity, to trace their connection with other elements of knowledge, their adaptation to the purpose for which they profess to have been given, their course in history, their influence over mankind; but let it not with a profane pride and vaulting ambition leap into the seat of their Eternal Author, and dictate what should and what should not have entered into a Revelation the fulness and clearness of which can be known, only as we know the human darkness and despair which it came to remove.

I have run this general outline only to open the way for considering a specific obligation especially incumbent upon us in view of the issue with which I am dealing. As it is not merely the tendency, but the avowed aim of the now reigning schools of thought to magnify the intellect*, some, as we have seen, in one way and some in another: and thus to encourage the fundamental vice of Individualism : so it is manifestly our duty—the duty of the Pulpit, the duty of Christian scholars—the duty of all who

* See Note 4.

bear office at the great centres of learning where the young life of the day is being moulded, to scrutinize more carefully than ever before the real powers and attainments of the human mind: what it can do and what it cannot; how far it can go and where it must stop; and especially to show its inability to solve the problems distinctively and exhaustively handled by Revealed Religion. Doubtless this has been done to some extent in every age. But it must be done again and by methods which the intellectual spirit of the time will be compelled to respect. We must move upon the same lines of inquiry, use the same appliances for moderating the claims of the individual reason that have been employed for its undue exaltation. We have special advantages for executing this task. The history of thought furnishes abundant materials for it. It is scarcely possible for philosophy to invent any new method of investigation, or reason to discover any new law of evidence or of demonstration. Every leading type of thought has run its round, exhausted its contents, and put itself on record beyond the possibility of essential change. The most sanguine advocate of the fresh and undeveloped possibilities of knowledge will not claim that much more light is likely to be thrown either upon the science that notes and arranges the facts of consciousness, or upon the science that deals with the essential reality of being, or upon the science that mediates between them and seeks to bring them into unity. Whether we regard them separately, or in combination, their results are before us. New thinkers may revise and readjust them, adding here and there fresh guesses and speculations: but they will be only as successive artists painting the same faces or the same scenes that the great masters have already glorified by their genius.

The results, I have said, are with us—results which a scholarly and comprehensive induction can mass together for examination whenever needed. And what do these tell us about the actual attainments of the human mind, not generally, but specifically, within the domain of Religion? The mind has been appealed to as the source and test of truth in four ways under which all modes of appeal may be grouped; viz. the sensational, the intuitive, the emotional and the reflective. Each of these functions or aspects of the mind has been not only analysed and catechised; but almost broken upon the wheel by the resolute and almost passionate spirit of modern inquiry in order to extort from it every mute sign or articulate word touching the buried secret of its real or its possible knowledge. And what has come of it? What is the testimony already filed away in the archives of thought? Briefly, this,—that the consciousness of man however questioned or however developed, whether on one side or on all sides, whether on the surface or in the depths, declares that it can neither create nor dispense with Religion; that Religion is a necessity and that itself is a riddle without it: and yet that it has no power to construct a Religion that will satisfy its own want, or endure its own criticism*; that it can neither determine the particular elements that should enter into Religion, nor the method by which they can be organized into a living whole; that it is at variance with itself in regard to the number and validity of its own intuitions; that it can neither altogether follow nor altogether desert the logic of reflective reason: because, on the one hand, it must formulate itself according to the necessary laws of thought, if it is to speak at all: and, on the other hand, if it so

* See Note 5.

formulate itself, it trips and stumbles helplessly in the meshes of inevitable logical contradictions. Surely these are very serious—if not fatal disabilities in a faculty that assumes not only to construct the subjective basis of Religion, but to exercise a supreme and determinate judgment upon the contents of a Religion avowedly revealed to it, because of its proved incompetency either fully to explain or fully to provide for its own want.

But the case becomes still stronger, if we take into account the failures of the reflective reason both on its speculative and on its practical side. These failures are all the more significant, because the religious consciousness, divorced from the reflective reason, is *ipso facto* excluded from the sphere of rational argument as applied either to the substance, or to the form, or to the external credentials of Religion. Now there is ample ground for affirming that reason on its speculative side, and regarded as the faculty for apprehending necessary truth or the Real in its highest sense, has yet accomplished "no absolute and unaltering solution of any problem peculiar to its sphere*." Even its *a priori* demonstrations of the existence of God are in a chronic

* See Note 6.

state of quarrel, resembling the members of a household divided against itself*. The old issue between phenomenalist and realist is no sooner fought out on one line, than it is renewed on another. The strife is endless and incurable. It goes on to-day just as though the host of great thinkers over whose graves it has marched had settled nothing except the fact that a settlement is hopeless. Systems rise and fall with the great tidal waves of thought whose ebb and flow are as inexplicable as they are inevitable. It is pitiful to recall the giant struggles, the vast outlays of mental force involved in the construction of these systems, and yet to be obliged to feel that the toil of Sisyphus and the thirst of Tantalus were not more hopeless.

But reason on its moral side and viewed as the faculty that determines the *ought* and the *ought not* has, on its own ground and working by itself, succeeded little better. Apart from the *much* that it has borrowed knowingly and the *still more* that it has borrowed unknowingly from Christianity, how little has it done toward discovering or certifying the essential facts—the fundamental principles of theo-

* See Note 7.

retical or practical Ethics, whose chief aim is not the formation of moral rules or moral sentiments, but the formation of character, the discipline of life! I honor more than I can express the profound study and the vast erudition of the noble company who have toiled on the foundations or on the superstructure of Ethical Science. But is it not true—am I mistaken in affirming that they have not as yet lifted out of the realm of controversy, so far as reason is concerned, the root question of the ultimate ground of moral obligation: and consequently the kindred question of a perfect standard of moral duty? If they have declared the right, they have discovered no sufficient motive power, no moral or spiritual dynamics that would lead the average of mankind to do it. It is certain that they have uttered no positive, unanimous word in regard to the comparative excellence and superiority of the several groups of virtues, *i.e.* the heroic, the amiable, the holy; and so have been unable to construct the perfect man in idea, far less in reality. Finally, while they have established the psychological supremacy of the conscience, they have not established its moral infallibility. They have proved that it was ordained to reign as chief and governor over all other faculties of man: but they have not proved that its authority extends over all moral truth offered to it from without—a fact, I may add, of primary moment in itself, but of special force just now, in view of the grounds on which the so-called liberal thought of the day has assailed the Catholic doctrine of the Atonement.

Divines have been faulted because they have spoken and written with so much freedom and assurance on the existing, actual state of the human heart without attempting to inquire into the original structure of man's moral nature. But metaphysical and ethical writers may be faulted quite as much, because they have confined themselves to an investigation of the moral constitution of man and a development of the moral faculty, without inquiring into the present state of the heart, or into the present working of the conscience as affected by the whole moral nature, *as it now is*. They tell us what the conscience was intended to be and to do: but tell us almost nothing of the conscience *as it is* amid the disorder and corruption both of the outward and inward life of man. Now it would seem as though the fact that the conscience has not the control that

it ought to have, that somehow it does not do its
appointed work, but bears itself not seldom like a
discrowned sovereign in the midst of its own empire,
is as worthy of investigation and explanation as its
original functions. The philosophers have carefully
avoided this side of the subject, as though afraid to
face the consequences, or as though conscious of their
inability to explain them, without being betrayed into
admissions or implications that would prove fatal to
the symmetry or the soundness of their theories.

After noting this fact, it only needs to be added
that nothing is more certain in the whole range
of ethical inquiry than that the very principles
arrived at by moral science, if fully adopted and
fairly applied in the very field which the philosophers have declined to enter, will conduct to
conclusions in regard to the corruption of man's
nature identical with those derived from the study
of God's Word. And these identical conclusions,
while they establish the intended authority of
conscience as an internal ruler, disprove its infallibility as a criterion of all moral truth that may
be presented to man by external authority. And
if this be true, then is the individual mind no

more the measure of all things demanding its assent
in virtue of its strictly moral, than of its strictly
intellectual faculties *.

In what has been said on this branch of my
subject, I have attempted only an outline (and
that a very general one,) of what I conceive to
be the proper and wholesome line of teaching in
our efforts to curb the ultra spirit of Individualism,
so far as it springs from certain admitted intellectual
tendencies of the day †. No doubt this kind of
gospel within the domain of metaphysical and
ethical inquiry will prove unpalatable to many with
whom we have to deal. No doubt those who need it
most will be least likely to heed it. The only
question with us, however, is whether it be true.
If it be so, then the urgencies of the hour require
us to insist upon it with increased energy of conviction. We have a duty not only to the wayward
whom we would reclaim; but yet more toward the
teachable and reverent among us who have not
yet broken from the old paths of faith and culture.

* See Note 8.   † See Note 9.

SERMON III.

1 Corinthians vii. 10, 11.   Colossians iii. 20.
Romans xiii. 1.   Ephesians iii. 9, 10.

Let not the wife depart from her husband..........And let not the husband put away his wife.

Children obey your parents in all things; for this is well pleasing unto the Lord.

Let every soul be subject unto the higher powers: for there is no power but of God; the powers that be are ordained of God.

And to make all men see what is the fellowship of the mystery, which from the beginning of the world hath been hid in God, who created all things by Jesus Christ: To the intent that now unto the principalities and powers in heavenly places might be known by the Church the manifold wisdom of God.

HAVING treated of the attitude to be assumed in Theology and Philosophy toward Individualism, I proceed to consider some of the grounds of opposition to it supplied by Institutions essential to the discipline and well-being of man. It is not unlikely that what I have urged as expedient and needful in our teaching within the precincts of Theology and Philosophy may have failed to command the assent of some. But I trust all will admit the gravity and force of the testimony to be drawn from this side of the subject. The current teaching of late years respecting the true nature and functions of the Family, the State, and the Church has, I fear, not been sufficiently bold and explicit. As the course of events has, from time to time, admonished us of the growth of schools of thought more or less hostile to the Christian and rational conception of these Institutions, we may have broken out into strong words of dissent, or remonstrance. Our fears may have been excited; perhaps, our indignation may have been aroused. But certainly there have been too few thoroughly earnest, thoroughly Christian, thoroughly reasoned attempts to re-examine, under the light of present facts, and to build up afresh

on its own indestructible foundations the great
argument touching the Divine and unchangeable
elements in these Ordinances, or their intended
mastery over the individual will. Somehow, while
the shadow of the enemy has been creeping stealthily
toward us, tongues that ought to have spoken at the
centres and along the highways of life have not
spoken as they might and should. The chief men in
Israel and in the seats of Sacred learning have either
underrated or mistaken the omens of the time;
or, understanding them, have been deluded by a false
security. Time is not allowed me: and, if it were, I
should distrust my ability to handle the argument
with suitable vigor and clearness. I can now do no
more than briefly allude to some of the hinges on
which it turns, and so invite to its consideration a
wider learning and a deeper logic.

As was stated in my first Discourse, it is asserted
by the more outspoken, as well religious as purely
sceptical, type of Individualism that, whatever organizations there may be external to the individual, he
possesses rights superior to them all—that as "he
comes to a clearer sense of the powers within him," he
is to give less and less heed to them—that the living

soul is the true Lord of all—that "as its needs may determine, Institutions of every sort are to increase, diminish, or totally disappear"—"that its power over them is that of the potter over the clay, either moulding them to its purpose, or, if it suit the soul better, breaking them under its foot." "As the conditions of man's life change, Christianity gives the individual authority to change the institutions in which his faith is enshrined; creeds and ordinances conformable to one age may not be so to the next; and he is to judge how far and in what direction they need modification. The right of adding to, or taking from them, is given by God into his hands *." These varied expressions of the same idea, so far from being imaginary or hypothetical, are the very language of a reputable school of Divines. They are repeated and intensified by hundreds of professedly Christian teachers in Great Britain and in America.

To make sure that I am not overstating the drift of the hour, let me put beside these statements the emphatic and pointed utterance of the now best known and most influential sceptical writer of England.

* Scotch Sermons. (Macmillan and Co. 1880.)

Speaking of the State and inclusively of every other organization exercising authority over the individual, he says, " Government being simply an agent, employed in common by a number of individuals to secure to them certain advantages, the very nature of the connection implies that it is for each to say whether he will employ such an agent or not. If any one determine to ignore this mutual safety confederation, nothing can be said except that he loses all claim to its good offices and exposes himself to the danger of maltreatment *."

Now it is impossible that any mind could hold such notions of the Church or of the State, unless it had first come to regard the former as the mere accidental embodiment of certain spiritual ideas, and therefore in all its parts and functions as shorn of every vestige of a Divine polity; and the latter as either a necessary evil, or an artificial and fortuitous resultant of historical contingencies, or as a mere instrumentality for enforcing justice between man and man, or as a simply economic society; and therefore, in any case, a thing founded on force, or in the individual's sense of expediency, or on the

* Herbert Spencer's "Social Statics," p. 229.

purely speculative basis of the social contract, or in the shifting impulses and judgments of popular sovereignty. These are not the doctrines, let us understand, of merely abstract thinkers who speak only to those shut up within cloistered walls. They are not confined to books or speeches addressed only to the few. They are floating about in the air. They are in your workshops and factories, in the resorts of your trades-unions, and in the tracts and papers that go into the hands of the million. They crop out in the resolutions and platforms of political agitators and socialistic propagandists. They are in the heads and hearts of tens of thousands who are already, or soon will be, wielding the power of the ballot. With such seed already in the ground, who can wonder at the harvest fast ripening for the sickle?

It is believed by many who look below the surface that the higher ends of the State are in danger of being sacrificed to gratify the sense of power, the passion for political control in the multitude. It is generally conceded that our time is engrossed in the consideration of rights rather than of duties, of powers rather than of responsibilities, of individual advancement rather than of what will make for the purity of Family life, for the true greatness of Society, and for the divinely ordered glory of the Church. Wise men sorrow as they look out over our modern life and see how the old cardinal virtues of reverence, humility, obedience, thankfulness, adoring trust are at a discount; while self-sufficiency, self-aggrandizement, "covetousness which is idolatry," ambition to master the world and to wring from it larger tribute to man's power and pleasure are at a premium. There is no mystery about it. These traits have not leaped to the front in some spasm of popular caprice or passion; rather are they the slowly-ripened fruit of teachings as false to the truth, as they have been persistent and deliberate in their utterance: and I may add that there is neither hope nor chance of giving them a check, except by the power of principles which they have only half stated, or openly perverted, or ignorantly denied. What then are these principles? In stating them there is no room for invention or discovery. What they always have been as matters of fact, that they are to-day, and that they will be to the end of time. False theories have only obscured, not annulled them. It is the delusion of man that he can make what God only can make, and that things so made have not only their source, but their end in himself; when, from their very nature, they must begin and end in the purposes of Him who created man and nature and all being for Himself.

Organic life wherever it exists bears the sign manual of Omnipotence and completes itself only as it fulfils the divine idea out of which it sprang. It is the essential property of organic being that the whole exists before the parts; not the parts before the whole; that the parts can grow only as they are shaped, co-ordinated, and combined by the life-principle working in and through the whole. Now the Family, the State, and the Church are in this sense organic wholes. Each of them antedates and outlasts its individual parts. Each, as embodying and applying the necessary laws of human development, precedes the individual and provides the conditions apart from which the individual could not realize a developed personality. Man can come to manhood only as he is integrated in consciousness and character by Institutions which are God's workmanship as truly as himself is. This is true of the Family and the State in the natural order and of the Church in the supernatural. It is well-nigh impossible, certainly it is at best a visionary abstraction, to conceive of the individual outside his necessary relations to these Divinely established fellowships. He can realize himself only through what is other than himself; and, speaking generally, it is only by the negation or surrender of his own individual self to a larger self, that he comes to know the meaning of himself as a spiritual being. To be true to the actual, as well as ideal order of rational life, we must reach the idea of any one of these organic Institutions, whether the Family, or the State, or the Church, not by first supposing a number of human beings—each complete in himself, and then by combining them to form the Institutions; but we must first think, conceive the Institutions in order to know the individuals. "The abstract, isolated individual is only the possibility of an existence which has never become actual." This, it may be said, is sound principle, good philosophy, when we think out the fundamental basis, the essential nature of the relations of the individual to the Family and the State; but how about its application to the Church? The question

is timely and in these days every way most pertinent. It invites an answer that, if it be valid,
involves inferences of the gravest moment in themselves, and of the utmost value as correctives of
much of the faulty thinking now prevalent on the
polity and authority of the Church.

Now if it be necessary in order to understand
aright the nature of the individual, to take into
account other finite beings and his relations to them ;
and if the whole nature of the individual can be
developed only in virtue of the organic character of
these relations ; still more necessary is it, if we would
know the meaning of man's nature, that we take into
account that Infinite and Absolute Being who is at
once the presupposition and the end of all finite
thought and life, and the relations of the individual
soul to that Being. And still further, if man's relations
to his fellow-men—the relations on which his life
and growth essentially depend—are concentrated in
and vitalized by organic wholes—*i.e.* the Family and
the State which are ordained and constituted of God ;
then, *a fortiori*, man's revealed and supernatural
relations to God, on which his yet higher life and
growth depend, must take shape and become operative

in and through a spiritual organism that was also ordained and constituted of God and equally adapted to its purpose. Now we believe and affirm the Church to be that organism : and, if it be, then its life must be an organic life; and, if organic, then composed of something more than a message to man, a divine idea, a moral force—something more than its individual human parts, or its individual supernatural gifts—even a body besides, the essentials of whose order, worship, faith are as divinely prearranged and established as the body itself. I deal with a fact. Were I to attempt its explanation, I should be led up at once to the central doctrine of Christianity—the Incarnation—which shows how, in the Divine counsel and in history, the fact was reached.

Here, then, in these Institutions, as elsewhere in the universe, "the universal is the *prius* of the particular"—the organic whole of the individual. And yet the universal must not be conceived as having any reality apart from the particular, or the organic body apart from its members. The wholes integrate and are integrated by the parts. They at once feed and are fed by the individuals of which they are composed. Neither can subsist or attain perfection without the other. The personality of the individual and the collective personality of the whole are inter-dependent at every point in the circle of development which is common to both. Now these are not two different truths in mere ideal or logical correlation, but opposite sides of one and the same truth. Unity completes itself in plurality and plurality completes itself in unity, the one in the many and the many in the one. If this principle be grounded in truth, we can build on it and apply it in the two directions along which our thoughts will now move. It will prepare us to see in what respects the Family, the State, and the Church are above the individual—his masters, not his servants; and how they have a meaning and a purpose that transcend and, at the same time, include the meaning and end of the individual; while, on the other hand, it will enable us to see in what senses they are subservient to the individual and exist for his benefit.

In the old Hebrew conception the individual was merged in the family and the tribe, though a certain dignity was associated with him, because of the belief that God had made him for His own glory, and had chosen him as one among many through whom the

Divine promise was to be handed on through the
ages. In the Greek thought which best interpreted
that of the ancients outside of Judea, it was assumed
that the individual existed only for the State and
that the State alone existed as an end in itself.
Between them it assumed that there was a necessary
contradiction, and it solved the contradiction by the
suppression of the individual. "The Greek State acknowledged no moral and tolerated no legal limitation
to its power. The conduct and ordering of life as
well in the inward thoughts and affections as in the
outward vocations and pursuits of the individual was
immediately and absolutely in its hands."

In much of the political speculation and very
largely in the political practice of modern life, the
exact opposite has been held—the State being
regarded as existing only for the individual and
the individual alone existing as an end in himself.
It is by the disciples of this view that we are asked
to regard the State, and, by obvious inference, the
Church, as mere forms or agencies adopted by the individual for the promotion of his own ends, and therefore as artificial and temporary associations created
by the voluntary alliance of individuals and entirely

subservient to their interests. Now the old heathen thought was ignorant of, and the modern conceit has perverted or denied the one fact—the one grand truth of the Christian Revelation which alone could lift the State, and, when the time came for it, the Church and, with both, the individual into the unity of organic life in which each can be an end to itself in virtue of its own moral personality; and yet each in its own sphere be subservient to the welfare of its members. I mean the truth that God made man in His own image, and with it the other inseparable truth that this image was fully revealed only in the God-man, Jesus Christ, by Whom, working through His own Body—the Church, redeemed humanity was to be put in its true relations with all things on earth and in heaven.

But to come back to my purpose, let us inquire how the great Institutions of society at once rule and serve the individual—are their own end, and yet find another end in him. And first in the natural order of thought comes the Family.

(I) The Family is an ordinance of God and invested with an authority commensurate with the purpose for which it was ordained. Parents bear rule as God's own deputies, not by virtue of human law; and they so bear it that no external power can lawfully restrain its legitimate exercise. Their commission rests upon natural law re-enforced and expanded, as well as sanctified by the law of Revelation. They are authorized and required to discipline and educate the life born of their mutual incorporation as one flesh. Children are to serve and obey in all things, not because they are too weak to do otherwise; nor yet because to do so is the implied condition of food, shelter, and raiment; nor because of any animal or physical consideration whatever; but simply for the reason that it is of the essence of the Family that they should do so. It is the fruit of an instinctive obligation and is the spontaneous admission of an authority, which is the divinely-planted germ of all forms of authority to be obeyed, when the child shall develop into the man.

Again, the Family dominates the individual, whether man or woman, because the marriage-bond is more than a simple contract or legal covenant that may be set aside by mutual consent. It is a union so intimate and so vital that the parties to it become one by a continuous and reciprocal moral determination. Once formed, it is disseverable by passion, or caprice, or antipathy. It is lifted above private convenience or private preference. Fluctuations of desire, changes of motive, disappointment as to results, or as to personal gifts have no power to revoke it. It is ordained to bring new life into being and its obligations to that life are as irrevocable as that life itself. Now it is just at this—the most vital nerve-centre of social being—that advanced Individualism delivers some of its worst assaults. It is insisting more and more upon a view of marriage that resolves it into a contract, the conditions of which are to be determined solely by the parties to it. In effect it declares love to be the only sacrament that can bind either husband or wife to stand fast in a plighted faith, and when love wanes or dies, the oath of life-long fidelity perishes with it. It has multiplied the grounds of divorce to such an extent that, now and then, even the civil courts that pass upon them have rebuked public opinion for not purging the statute-books of some of the American States of the demoralizing license of their laws. It holds that no man or woman should be forced to continue in a relation that has become repugnant or irksome; and that the tie is really binding only so long as it produces the happiness which the parties to it had a right to expect. And what is more, it holds these views of marriage quite consistently with its own fundamental principle—the satisfaction and welfare of the individual the one primary interest that dominates all others.

But further, the Family rules the individual, rises superior to his opinions, wishes, and volitions because of an inherent attribute of sacredness. Largely as this quality may proceed from Divine institution and enactment, it is quite as largely grounded upon the instincts and traditions of mankind in every age and in every land; and upon the universal conviction that the Family is the nursery of the Church and the Nation; and that on the whole, as is the Family, so will be the Church and the Nation. The depth and power of this conviction are attested by all history. Christianity emphasizes and confirms it by additional sanctions; but does not create it. It is as old and as wide as the human race, and prevails as a central fact in its art, literature and laws, as well as in its various religions. The first book of Holy Scripture records not only the foundation, but the dignity and sacredness of the Family. " The Iliad, in which there is the most vivid reflection of the spirit of archaic life, is the story of a war in vindication of the purity of the marriage-bond; and its heroes are those who go to battle to avenge the violated sanctity of the Family; the Æneid is the story of filial duty and reverence. In Greece, its earliest institutions—the *phratriæ* and *gentes*—are the evidences of the power and dignity of the Family." In Rome the sacredness of the marriage-tie affirmed itself in many of the observances of its religion and in the characteristic tone of its laws; while in that most populous and enduring of empires, China, filial reverence and obedience have beyond all else proved the cohesive and conservative force of society and of the nation. So true is this that it is an accepted law of history, almost a recognized axiom of social ethics, that communities and nations are doomed to corruption and overthrow so soon as they begin to impair the sacredness, or to loosen the obligations of domestic life. And it is equally a law of history that communities and nations, when they begin to do this, uniformly begin by gradually ceasing to uphold the sacredness of the Family as a moral order having an end in itself as well as beyond itself; and as uniformly conclude by treating it as a thing devised by men, grounded on the law of expediency, and maintained or dissolved as the will of the individual may determine *.

But if, in all these senses, the Family must govern the individual and assert its superiority over him, there are others in which it must serve him and be subordinated to his interests. He has a right to hold it strictly to its own commission and to demand from it all that it was intended to do for him. In virtue of his personality he, too, has an end in himself. He must be treated as more than an instrument or a slave. He bears God's image and is marked for an eternal as well as a temporal life. His franchises match his hopes and keep pace with his capabilities. He is to be educated into a consciousness of the larger life of the State and the yet larger one of the Church. He is to be so tutored and fashioned as to develop into the twofold and yet homogeneous character of the citizen-Christian and the Christian citizen. He has not only a body to be reared, but

* See Note 10.

a soul, a mind, a heart to be instructed, so that to him the highest freedom will be the service of truth and righteousness. Such are the claims of the individual upon the Family, and the Family serves the individual in all offices necessary to the satisfaction of these claims. The mastery of the individual over the Family is the mastery of rights founded in the nature of things and the constitution of humanity. The reciprocal mastery of the Family over the individual has the same foundation, and the two masteries are the integration of an organic life which precedes and excels every other organism in its influence over man.

(II) Turning now to the State or the Nation, I am to show that it does not exist for the individual as its exclusive end; that it is not only greater than the individual because of its greater power and duration; but by reason of its own inherent constitution— its own aims, labors and achievements. In speaking of the State, I shall speak of it in its essential idea, and not in its accidents—as imperial, monarchical, republican, or democratic. I shall assume, moreover, (what some may think needs to be proved), that it is ordained of God, that it has a conscious, continuous,

responsible personality *; and therefore a moral as
well as a political life, that it may do right and be
rewarded, and that it may sin and be punished, that
it may live its own life, conform to its own law,
do its own work, act after its own methods, be self-
determining; and yet that it is God's instrument
for purposes that can be attained in no other way,
and that its noblest liberty consists in the voluntary
acceptance of God's way.

It is of the essence of personality that whatever
other ends it may have, it must have an end in and
for itself. But the Nation has personality and this
personality expresses itself "first in the consciousness,
then in the conscience of the people in whom it is
constituted," and finally through its own self-centred
will. But if the State or the Nation possess this
attribute, it must have ends of its own which, though
coincident with the interests of the individual as far
as those interests extend, sweep out indefinitely
beyond them. After it has done serving the individual; after it has defined and protected his rights;
after it has indicated and enforced his duties; it
also serves the race. True it is that all such higher

* See Note 11.

service has its reflex benefits for the individual; but primarily the individual is not the aim of that higher service and its benefits to him are only indirect and consequential.

Again, that the State has not the individual for its chief or exclusive end is shown by the fact that, though political in the mode of its organization and activity, its noblest function is to represent and advance the moral order of the world, to give practical force in the secular relations of man to the laws that constitute that order, to witness in each bounded sphere of its sovereignty for universal justice and eternal truth; and so to be in virtue of a natural ordination and on its own side of human life not only a king to bear rule, but a prophet to teach, and a priest to offer sacrifice—even the sacrifice of unselfish service and devotion first to humanity and through humanity to God. The State is not in itself a righteous power; and yet in its normal idea and after its own manner as a representative and witness of the world's moral order, it cannot, if true to its own noblest end, but work for righteousness. History shows the process by which humanity is developed according to the Divine purpose, and

the life of the Nation is, next to the life of the
Church, the highest manifestation of that process.
Indeed, as all organic instrumentalities working in or
upon man have their origin in the one eternal
purpose of God; so, at some point in the wide circuit
through which they travel, they must meet and
coalesce both in aims and results as the final
consummation of that purpose.   They have one
beginning; they must have one end.   And as their
beginning attested the unity of God, so must they by
their historic work first vindicate that unity amid the
world's fractures and anarchies; and then, at last, as
their end, proclaim it as restored and established
forever, that all things may be gathered together in
one and God may be all in all.   If this be so, then it
is the deepest idea of the State, as it is the foremost
end of the State, while not formally a righteous
power, to speak, after its own sort, for that same
moral order that the Church supernaturally and more
articulately voices by its faith, worship and sacraments.   If it were not so, then the only ground of its
authority as the source and administrator of positive law would be either force, or expediency, or an
implied compact, or the will of majorities.   The State

is what it is because it is a moral before it is a political power, or a political power only that it may become a moral one; and in either case its end is realized only as it passes up into unity with the Divine purpose as manifested partially in history and wholly in Revelation.

Still again, the State, considered as equivalent to the Nation, rises above the individual, quite loses sight of him in its connection with races. It is the chief outlet and interpreter of race instincts, race aspirations, race energies. Civilization at large looks to the Nation to mediate between it and the race-characteristics of mankind. Some study history by the light of great names that cannot be recalled without recalling the peoples and eras to which they belonged. Some read it by the key found, as they believe, in the properties of races. Still others find in nations, not in races, the integral powers in history; and this is the view now taken by the best thought of our time. The Nation combines and fuses into unity of temperament and purpose the peculiarities not merely of this or that race, but of all races drawn within its borders. Races as such have no status in the political or moral order. They neither sow nor

reap, build nor destroy. If they may be said to
have missions, errands, destinies, these cease to be
ideas and become realities only as they are worked
out under the conditions of national life. It is in
and through the State that what is only half
conscious and indeterminate in the race is developed
into the force and dignity of definite motives and
definite objects. The only points of contact, therefore, between races and the general body of civilization are and must be essentially national.

But there is still another and more impressive
illustration of the manner in which the life of the
State sweeps widely out beyond all individual interest
to be drawn from that, perhaps, most commanding
function in virtue of which the Nation gathers up, con-
serves, and transmits the cumulative results of human
effort. Individuals, like shadows, come and go. Even
the centuries looked at, one by one, are fugitive, and
in their onward march bear with them passively and
uncritically the forces that have wrought within
them. The Nation alone is, in the world's order,
the continuous and conscious factor; and because
continuous and conscious, capable of blending together in an unbroken unity the wisdom and repose

of the past with the hope and aspiration of the future. Whatever the growth of language, science, law, literature, art, physical discovery, civil government, social experience; whatever the fruits of the toil and sacrifice of the great and good who have won a lasting hold on the memory of mankind; or of the unremembered labor and suffering of the unhonoured and unknown in all humbler walks of life; whatever may have been achieved in any age or in any land by acts of piety, bravery, love, denial too obscurely done to be sung by poets or recorded by historians—all find in the Nation's life not only an ample storehouse for their safe-keeping, but a discriminating and responsible trustee, an incorporated and majestic intelligence to collect and preserve them. This deep, broad life, impelled by instinct as well as by reason, deems not its duty done in merely accepting as an inheritance such priceless treasures. It knows that it is not to keep them as talents wrapt in a napkin and buried in the ground, but as living powers to be sent forth on fresh errands and into fresh fields of action. Thus it not only receives, but enriches what it receives; not only bears itself as the heir of all the ages, but as a wise steward who makes the most of the trust committed to him in the interest of the posterities to come. But admirable and comprehensive as is this function of the State; high as it lifts the State above the individual, it is not so general or so remote as to belong of right to the abstract and ideal rather than to the practical. For though it demonstrates the fact that the Nation has other ends than those bounded by individual interests; it also proves how beneficently the State works for the individual, while pursuing ends that manifest and uphold the corporate continuity of the race. And it does so in this wise.

"No man can think of his own separate individual life without a certain sad, almost bitter feeling of its shallowness and brevity. So much of it seems abortive, that he is tempted to take refuge in petty cares that will relieve him of all sense of incongruity in the littleness of life. Noble designs, why should he cherish them when time is not given to fulfil them? Unselfish enthusiasm for the progress of mankind in truth and goodness, why should he allow himself to be swept on by its fervor and energy, when soon and forever he shall cease to have any more part in all that is done beneath the sun ? Visions of perfection and glory for himself to be realized only after immeasurable toil, denial and doubt, why should he not banish them from his soul as tantalizing intruders, when a few more years shall bury himself and them in a common grave" ? The beginnings and materials of great things are within him; but they are never realized; and the higher his ideals soar the more they disclose the poverty and meanness of actual life. Everywhere boundless possibilities have their counterpart in miserable performances. All this indeed does not trouble much the bulk of mankind, bent, as they are, upon little else than the satisfaction of animal wants and selfish desires; but to highly cultured and aspiring minds—to commanding, originative intellects—to heroic or saintly spirits—to souls hungering for truth and righteousness—to wills that, in their passionate yearning to do and dare for all that is best and purest, strive to push back these cramping limitations of time—to all such this is a deep and bitter experience. The remedy, as we all know, is commonly found in the Christian view of the soul's immortality; and this ought to be effective with all who accept it as an article of their faith. But there

L. S.   11

are many who do not accept it as a living, habitual motive; and yet who are capable of doing very precious and needful work for their fellowmen. And it is these that the State may inspire with hope and courage by holding up to them as a practical motive an inferior and vague, but still, after its kind a noble immortality—nobler than that offered by the materialism of the day, the immortality of matter and force—nobler than that to which the pantheist would lure us, the immortality of absorption in the Infinite Unknown—nobler, too, than that carved out for us by the idolaters of reason, the immortality of ideas. To the individual fretting himself into despair, or wasting himself in indolence under the sense of his own feebleness and littleness: here, says the State, is a life—the life of a great, growing, continuous personality—the Nation's own life built up out of all that is left of the ages that have gone, and holding in itself the prophecy of what is to be in the ages to come—a life into whose bone and fibre have been transmuted and assimilated what poets have sung, and wise men have taught, and statesmen, lawmakers, warriors and patriots have achieved; and besides whatever all the nameless millions have done for God and humanity: accept the vocation, seize the opportunity it offers you. Come forth from your isolation and open your heart to its wide sympathies and aspirations. Learn from it your place and your work not only in the fellowship of your country; but also in the grander brotherhood of mankind. Wherever you toil, whether in the retreats of learning or in the crowded areas of trade and industry, or out on the skirmish line of the battle against error and wrong; whether in high places or low ones; whether in wealth or poverty; know certainly that, in that larger life, nothing you say or do worthy to be remembered shall be lost or forgotten. Eminently true of the Church, it is also quite as true in its degree of the State that, as God has provided some better thing for us that our fathers without us should not be made perfect; so He has provided some like better thing for our children that, we without them, should not be made perfect. It is this law that ennobles our imperfect life; because it certifies, in every such vanishing individual life, the promise of a future without which it cannot be made perfect.

Thus the State, while working for ends above and beyond the individual, becomes a heritage for the individual. "The wealth of its historical associations and the grandeur of its historical epochs are its gifts. The majesty of its law and the authority of its government and its conquering power are around him; its acquisitions are his vantage ground, its domain is his home; its order is his working field; its rights are his armour; its achievements are the heights he treads; its freedom the ampler air he breathes;" while more to be desired than all—its larger, profounder, mightier life lives in his life, levelling it up step by step to the magnanimity of its own spirit and the greatness of its own aims.

(III) Finally, I pass on to speak of the Church as affected by the root principle of Individualism. Were not the proofs at hand, we might well deem it incredible that, in an age of so much intelligence and with more than an average of knowledge of Gospel teaching and ecclesiastical history, such sadly defective views of the origin and constitution of the Church should be held in any quarter, as those to which I am about to allude. Anarchical and destructive as may be the notions touching the Family and the State now propagated by the advanced schools of Individualism, the full extent of their wild and pernicious tendency crops out only when we consider their bearing on the Church, the foremost of the Institutions commissioned of God for the education and redemption of man. It is here that they open up chasms in the immemorial tradition of Catholic truth, that may well startle us and compel us to ask, whereunto these things may grow?

If what we are told be true, we must at once and absolutely abandon our faith in the Divine origin and supernaturally developed structure of the Church; and drop to the level of accident, expediency, convenience. The one Body breaks up and dissolves, and only the one Spirit remains. Christianity evaporates into ideas, sentiments, tendencies. It ceases to be a visible, historic kingdom, and is thinned away into a spiritual force that organizes itself throughout the entire domain of its action according to the haphazard suggestions of individual leaders, or of particular schools of religious opinion, or according to the supposed requirements of each succeeding generation. This, I say, is the notion that we must accept with all its inferences, if what we are told be true.

And what, specifically, are we told? Why that as "the Sabbath was made for man, not man for the

Sabbath": and that, in regard to all ecclesiastical Ordinances, as every man is justified in applying to himself, by reason of his inherent dignity and moral birth-right, the very words applied by the adorable Saviour to Himself—"In this place there is one greater than the temple": so the Church, with all its institutions for teaching and discipline, with all its sacramental channels of grace and bonds of fellowship was made solely *for* man; and is, therefore, alterable by man; exists for man's benefit as its highest end; and, therefore, must take on whatever form, cast aside, as a worn-out garment, whatever rite, prerogative, creed, or ministration he may decree. Historically, it must, in short, in all save its central idea, be the ever changing outgrowth of man's own conception of his wants. A liberty is his of which no authority can despoil him to determine, at any moment, how much or how little of the Church may be needful to himself: and whether he will dwell within or without its fellowship, according as he may judge it to be a help or a hindrance to his spiritual life.

But if such liberty be his, (and it is now confidently asserted that it is), then it follows of necessity that the Church is not an organic body, but a mere aggregation of individuals: not a kingdom framed, established, equipped of God, changeless in its structural essentials as the message it delivers: but a voluntary society endowed with an indefeasible right to determine its own organization, and with that its own conditions of membership both as to faith and discipline.

And to realize how closely this issue concerns us, it is well to remember that it must be met within our own Christian lines. It is thrust upon us not more by open antagonists, than by nominal friends who, strangely enough, seem not to be surprised or restrained by the fact that this conception of the Church has the hearty sympathy of minds to whom the very names of Gospel, Church, Sacrament, Ministry, Creed, are an intellectual nuisance, or a moral impertinence. Brethren, it were a crime in us to ignore, or to underrate the depth and breadth of this controversy. Would we have the Gospel? We must defend its ordained witness and interpreter. Would we have the New Testament and hand it on as we received it? We must resist, as with one will and one heart, this attempt to sap and mine the corporate unity and historic continuity of the Body that originally framed and certified, and, during all the Christian centuries, has preserved and transmitted its Canon. Would we continue to worship the Triune God, and to preach, and to baptize, and to distribute to the faithful the bread of life after the manner of our fathers? Then, too, after their manner, must we witness a good confession in this solemn matter as against all gainsayers of Zion's glory: and this, though like an anvil we be hammered by organized dissent, or beaten with rods, like some alien captive, by a liberalism that believes itself stronger without than with organization.

As to the answer to this and all similar errors, the occasion limits me to the utmost brevity of statement. Would that the Word of God were as full and explicit on all subjects touched by it, as it is on this. If anything in it is declared to be absolutely of God and not of man, it is the Church. It was the fulfilment of His purpose, the creation of His will, the revelation of His wisdom and love. There has never been an hour since the Fall that it did not exist. Through all the ages it has been doing its appointed work, has had its Creed, its Ordinances, its Worship, its Priesthood. There have been no changes in its essential elements save such as have grown out of and corresponded with God's own successive dispensations, God's own advancing revelations of "the mystery of godliness." Patriarchs, prophets, lawgivers, kings have been its ministers, and all of them were called and sent of God, not of man. In the fulness of time, the Church of old fulfilled, finished, merged itself in Christ, the one Mediator between God and man, the promise of Whom it had borne through the ages. Gathered up in Him, its life principle—its organic energy interfused and blended with His incarnate Godhead and by it intensified, enriched, enlarged according to the eternal purpose of the Father, it issued from Him again for its work in history, in a way faintly figured to us by water flowing from its springhead or light from the sun. When He declared, "Upon this rock I will build my Church*," He declared that He would build in time, and out of, and among men that which was already in life, in power, and in purpose, *as well as in form*, in Himself and one with Himself. The actual building began with the descent of the Spirit and was visibly manifested

* St Matt. xvi. 18.

by the preaching and baptizing of Peter on the Day of Pentecost; when, and afterward, "the Lord added to the Church daily such as should be saved *." Even this "adding," be it observed, as exhibiting the process of building, was so essentially God's and not man's act, that the Inspired Record is careful to say the Lord did it.

Such, briefly, was the origin of the Christian Church, and that origin in every important characteristic was radically different from the origin of any earthly society. It came into being, as everything bearing God's image and superscription in the organic and rational world comes into being—His own thought taking on the vesture woven of His own hand—His own life clothing itself with a body born of His own will and moulded after His own purpose. It came into being, too, not only according to God's method in the order of nature; but also according to God's method in the order above nature—the spiritual, supernatural order, in which He has contact with His work in a manner of which the bounded realm of mere antecedents and consequents affords us neither sign, nor figure, nor vaguest glimpse.

* Acts ii. 47.

But this view of the Church's outgrowth from Christ is greatly strengthened by what the Scriptures tell us concerning its actual structure. First, and as the simplest representation, we learn how it was planted as the least of all seeds, and, how developing after its own law, it was to grow until its branches covered the whole earth. Next, we learn how it rose under the hands of the master builders from its chief corner stone, Jesus Christ, "in Whom all the building fitly framed together groweth unto an holy temple in the Lord*." Though both these conceptions of growth involve the principle of organic development, and therefore imply an organic structure, and, if organic, then one whose end was present in its beginning, and whose whole was potentially prior to its parts; yet they also render it possible that the thing planted, or the thing builded might stand apart from the Being that planted or built it, having no necessary share in His personal life, deriving no quickening, continuous virtue from His wisdom and love, breathing its own air, compacted by its own joints, weaving its own tissues. But we are not allowed to stop here. Inspiration throbs with

* Eph. ii. 21.

another and deeper pulsation of thought, and its language rises to a loftier meaning. The Church is no longer only a *planted* or a *builded* thing; but is intensified and exalted into a *living body*, the fulness of Him that filleth all in all, whose Head is Christ "from Whom the whole body fitly joined together and compacted by that which every joint supplieth, according to the effectual working in the measure of every part, maketh increase of the body unto the edifying of itself of love*." Thus the growth and the Grower, the building and the Builder, the plant and the Planter, the Body and the Life that pulsates in the Body are one and inseparable. It is one and the same personality repeating itself by a double and yet identical manifestation. It is the one Christ once on earth, now in heaven, always abiding with us in vital continuity by the Spirit and in the Church, which is His Body indefectible, universal, immortal; not a mere construction by even a Divine Will-power, far less a society founded on an aggregation or union of individual wills; but a spiritual generation and outbirth of the eternal Godhead in Christ Jesus.

* Eph. iv. 16.

But if God's Word, in its account of the origin of the Church and of the evolution of its structure, discovers no trace of human suggestion; so, in its account of the ends for which the Church was instituted, it is careful to place not only its relations to God before its relations to man; but its work for God before its work for man. The individual soul so far from being its chief is always its secondary object. In all its functions it was needful that it should be the master, if, in any, it was to be the servant of man. In none is it amenable to man, in all it is responsible to God. It is impossible to study the ends for which the Church exists, as they are set forth in Revelation, without seeing that it has ends which immensely transcend the interests of mortals, and which, antedating the foundation of the world, will outlast its dissolution. Time in its widest reach hovers over and drops away from them like a shadow. Out of eternity they came forth and into eternity they return. At a point in their boundless sweep determined of God, man is taken up and redeemed; and at another likewise determined, he is left through endless ages with or without God, according as he has accepted or rejected the overtures of mercy.

The Scriptures do not leave us to infer from their general teachings, or from any indirect statement, how these ends of the Church are graduated in their hold upon man and upon things above and beyond him. The Apostle, in describing his errand as a preacher and Christ's errand as the Saviour of man, describes by necessary implication the chief ends of the Church; for preaching is one of the means by which the Church does its work, accomplishes its ends; and Christ's mission to the world is the Church's mission, because, as His Body and by His Spirit, it continues His mediatorial work. It was the burden of the Apostles' preaching, as it was the purpose of Christ's coming, "to make all men see what is the fellowship of the mystery, which from the beginning of the world hath been hid in God who created all things by Jesus Christ"; but then, immediately following this, is the yet higher end of both announced in words most significant and remarkable in this connection; namely, "to the intent, that now unto the principalities and powers in heavenly places might be known the manifold wisdom of God, according to the eternal purpose which he purposed in Christ Jesus *."

* Eph. iii. 10, 11.

Again, the Apostle preached to bring men "to the light of the knowledge of the glory of God in the face of Jesus Christ * :" that by this light they might be brought to see, "that God was in Christ reconciling the world unto himself†." But here, too, we have the higher and further end in the same Apostle's words—an end common to the Church and to the Truth it delivered, "that in the dispensation of the fulness of times He might gather together in one *all* things in Christ, both which are in heaven and which are on earth ‡."

Indeed, so definite and luminous is the witness of Holy Scripture on this point, that none who accept its authority can doubt that the Church exists for vastly wider and sublimer purposes than the salvation of the individual. What it does for him, great, unspeakably great as it is, is rather the beginning than the end of its work—a single event, or at most a single chapter in its record, rather than its sole function, or its exclusive task.

In the foregoing thoughts it has been furthest from my aim to dwarf the individual and to magnify institutions whether heavenly or earthly. In common

---

* 2 Corin. iv. 6.　　† 2 Corin. v. 19.　　‡ Eph. i. 10.

with all that love Him who gave Himself for us, and who, by that matchless gift, would enable every man to take his place in the scale of being as only a little lower than the Angels and to have dominion over all things beneath him, I rejoice at every fresh proof of his real greatness. So far from gainsaying what modern life has done for him; so far from narrowing or withholding any of his rights or privileges; so far from questioning the vast capabilities of his nature, or disparaging the range and power of his faculties, or doubting the destiny of glory that awaits him; I have only attempted to trace for him, by inference rather than by direct statement, the path of true progress, the law of all healthy development graven by God's hand at once and equally upon the individual and humanity at large; upon the Family, the State, and the Church.

In a time that has already done so much and promises to do still more for the elevation of the individual, it is not strange that he should be tempted to wander away, or, now and then, to shoot rashly from the orbit in which, by the ordinance of God and the laws of his own being, he must move, if he would not stifle his own energies, shatter his own hope, mutilate his own ideal. It has been my endeavour to lift from this orbit the shadows, nay, in some cases, the dark eclipse cast upon it by misleading speculations, exaggerated theories, and even favorite watchwords and rallying cries of the masses touching the rights and powers of the individual as defined and limited by those of the great organic Institutions whose authority is the authority of Him by Whom all things were made and in Whom all things consist.

That man must live in the by-ways, or in the clouds who does not see the deep, strong drift of the hour toward a yet larger liberty for the individual and a yet smaller area for authority *. It may or may not be the duty of the wise to resist it ; but certainly it is their duty—if there be poison in it, to extract it; if there be peril in it, to guard against it; if there be passion and violence in it, to restrain them ; if there be ignorance and unbelief in it, to enlighten them ; if there be spiritual death in it, to preach to it the one only Name given under heaven whereby we may be saved.

As in regard to the subject which has engaged our thought, so for all things affecting the interests

* See Note 12.

of sound learning and true religion, the purity
and sacredness of the Family, the order of Society,
the growth of the State, the administration of
Government, the welfare of mankind, the strength
and honor of the Catholic Church, the glory of
the Triune God—for all let us pray and work as
the very children of God and members of Christ,
waiting in humility and patience for the day "when
we shall all come into the unity of the faith, and
knowledge of the Son of God, unto a perfect man,
unto the measure of the stature of the fulness of
Christ*." Then, "in thinking God's thoughts we
shall be thinking our own; and in doing His will
we shall be doing our own"; and so shall taste the
only true freedom of a spiritual being. Individual
opinion shall vanish in the vision of eternal truth,
and Individual duty, in becoming the witness and
expression of Infinite love, shall become the most
ardent desire of the soul.

*Eph. iv. 13.

NOTES.

NOTE 1.

"Entire quarters of the globe, Africa and the East have never had, and have not yet the idea of free-will. The Greeks and Romans, Plato and Aristotle and the Stoics had it not. On the contrary they conceived only that a man by his birth (as Athenian or Spartan citizen &c.), or by strength of character, by education, by philosophy, only so did they conceive a man to be free. This idea came into the world through Christianity, in which it is that the individual, *as such*, has an *infinite* worth, as being aim and object of the love of God, and destined, consequently, to have his absolute relation to God as spirit, to have this spirit dwelling in him."

Hegel, *Philosophie des Geistes*, p. 374.

NOTE 2.

That I have not overstated this view, or the importance of meeting it, the following thoughts will prove. They are from a volume entitled "Scotch Sermons" 1880, (Macmillan and Co.), in whose Preface we read "This volume has originated in the wish to gather together a few specimens of a style of teaching, which increasingly prevails amongst the clergy of the Scottish Church." "It may serve to indicate a growing tendency, and to show the direction in which thought is moving." Substantially the same teaching on this point, *i. e.* the uselessness and obsoleteness of the External Evidences of the Christian Religion might be quoted from many sources (ecclesiastically) nearer home.

Says the preacher (p. 297) "Now we learn on reflection that evidence divides itself into two great classes, one of which naturally connects itself with the sacerdotal principle of religion, the other with the individualistic. That which is homogeneous with Sacerdotalism (?) refers as a rule to historical testimony, calls in the aid of empirical logic, and generally adopts the method of verification employed in science....Leaving out of view all philosophical objections to this mode, there is a practical one of very great force, which it is worth our while to consider. The objection is the want of success which this sort of evidence for religious truth has hitherto had in combating scientific scepticism. That it has been unsuccessful will probably not be admitted by the Christian controversialist. But the whole life both of man and nature will soon be the recognized domain of physical science, and then there will be seen more clearly than now the inability of religion to defend itself by the old empirical method. People will have to relinquish it altogether or discover a new basis for it, and uphold it by a more enlightened method. Let Christian apologists be ever so clever or so laborious, they will have to change their principles, ere they can make much way among the educated classes. I believe they will have to make trial of that form of evidence which connects itself with Individualism, whereof the principle is this : that religious truth is its own evidence, the spiritual consciousness the ultimate authority." Unfortunately even the adoption of the method here so strongly urged leads, according to the preacher, to a very sad and discouraging result. "The popular apologist ought to consider whether, fighting the battle of Christianity on an objective basis, he is not rather harming his cause than helping it." But if the battle be fought on the subjective basis, the result is quite as hopeless. "For the moment you bring the reasons for your belief from the depths of inner consciousness, and state them logically on paper, a thousand to one but they seem feeble to yourself,...and I am afraid if the spiritual ideas of the Bible do not commend themselves as true to the consciousness of those who read them, *there is no method at present by which they can be proved.* At all events, in the present state of popular culture, philosophical proof could not be made widely intelligible." Again, "the spectacle of the multitude looking to theology for evidence to support its faith is pathetic and even tragical. The evidence that theology is able to give is not in this age particularly valuable, and people should be taught, though with caution, to seek refuge from unbelief in their spiritual instincts." What makes the case even more hopeless, as the preacher admits, is the fact that these instincts are "so vague and inarticulate" that "we have no phraseology for them," and, therefore, cannot put into shape the sort of evidence they give. Each consciousness is shut up within itself and can neither give, nor receive any tangible help from the consciousness of any body else. So that what is evidence to one may be no evidence to another, and *vice versa.*

NOTE 3.

Protagoras was the best known and most influential of the Athenian Sophists. He was a disciple of Heraclitus—the originator of the philosophical notion of sensation as the source of knowledge and of the theory of the relativity of knowledge. He greatly expanded and, with much logical power, applied the fundamental doctrine of his master to the knowing subject—the individual mind. As a corollary from this doctrine, he asserted that Man is the measure of all things, of things that are that they are, of things that are not that they are not, πάντων χρημάτων μέτρον ἄνθρωπος, τῶν μὲν ὄντων ὡς ἐστί, τῶν δὲ οὐκ ὄντων ὡς οὐκ ἐστιν. Just as each thing appears to each man, so it is to him. All truth is relative. Plato discussed and refuted this thesis in his *Theaetetus,* in his Dialogue *Protag.,* and in his *Sophistes.* Aristotle handled it also (*Metaph.* III. 2. 32, p. 998).

Ueberweg (*History of Philosophy,* Vol. I. p. 75) says very aptly, "In illustration of the fundamental idea of Protagoras, a kindred utterance of Goethe may be compared, which will illustrate as well the relative truth of that idea, as the onesidedness of disallowing the objective reason." I have observed that I hold that thought to be *true* which is *fruitful for me*, which adjusts itself to the general direction of my thought, and at the same time furthers me in it. Now, it is not only possible, but natural, that such a thought should not chime in with the sense of another person nor further him, perhaps even be a hindrance to him, and so he will hold it to be false; when one is right thoroughly convinced of this he will never indulge in controversy (Goethe, *Zelterscher Briefwechsel*, v. 354).

Compare further the following in Goethe's *Maximen und Reflexionen:* "When I know my relation to myself and to the outer world, I say that I possess the truth. And thus each may have his own truth, and yet truth is ever the same."

NOTE. 4.

I cannot refrain from quoting in this connection a passage from Canon Liddon which is as eloquent as it is true. Uttered some seventeen years ago, the march of events and the more extreme development of certain schools of thought, during that time, have only served to give additional force to it. "Faith is proscribed by that undue exaltation of intellect which leaves no room for it. The great conflict which rages between the pride of natural intellect and the claims of faith is fought out on no remote or imaginary battle-field. And upon the issue to many a man who hears me may depend nothing less momentous than the salvation of his soul and his place in eternity....Think of it well, brethren, and take your parts. Believe it, there is a submission of thought which is not slavery, and there is a haughty mental independence which, alas! knows itself to be anything but true freedom. They do not really suffer defeat who make their submission to God : they who, while opposing Him, seem to conquer, can win but a perilous and short-lived victory. On this side is Paul, first a persecutor, then an Apostle ; and Justin, once a philosopher, then an Apologist and Martyr; and Augustine, who out of a sensualized heretic and free-thinker, is raised by Divine grace to be a Saint and Doctor of the Universal Church. On that side is Julian, Emperor and Apostate, with endowments of character and gifts of intellect so calculated to win our highest interest and admiration ; yet ending a reign in which rare accomplishments, and consummate address, and vast political power had been vainly employed against the Gospel with the despairing confession, 'Thou hast conquered, O Galilæan.' In this short life we see only a small portion of the full results of thought and action. But another world casts its shadow across our path ; and we often anticipate the endless future with a keen presentiment which is not less than tragical. Assuredly intellect has its rights, its privileges, its duties, its triumphs. But faith has likewise her own province and her unshared capacities; and while all around her is change and uncertainty, she gazes unfalteringly upon the Unseen and Eternal. She knows that for the Object on which her eye is fixed, all else, if need be, may well be sacrificed, since all else will one day pass away."

University Sermons, 2nd Edition, 1863—5, p. 181.

NOTE 5.

"All attempts hitherto made to construct a religion independent of Scripture have turned out acknowledged failures: the systems reared cannot stand a sifting examination by reason, and have been utterly powerless on human character. There was an expectation, long cherished by many, that something better than the old Christianity of the Bible literally interpreted might come out of the great German philosophic systems; but these hopes have been doomed to disappointment. The idea was fondly cherished by some that certain men of literary genius, who had caught more or less of the spirit of the German metaphysics, such as Coleridge, and Goethe, and Carlyle, must have something new and profound to satisfy the soul in its deeper cravings, could they only be induced to utter it. Coleridge has played out his tune sweet and irregular as the harp of Æolus, and all men perceive that he never had anything to meet the deeper wants of humanity, except what he got from the songs of Zion. It has long been clear, in regard to Goethe, and is now being seen in regard to Carlyle, that neither of them ever had anything positive to furnish in religion, and that all they had to utter was blankly negative, and the last hope of drawing anything soul-satisfying from these quarters has vanished from the minds of those who have been most impressed by their genius.

The school of intuitionalist divines, influenced by the Teutonic speculations, have given profound expositions of some of the deeper principles and feelings of the soul, and have thus furnished a contribution to philosophy, and incidentally benefited theology. It has erred, not in the positive views which the members of it have unfolded, but in what they have omitted and scornfully denied. In particular they have lost sight of one of the deepest and most ineradicable of all our intuitions : they have taken no notice of that sense of God and of a judgment-day which make men feel dissatisfied with every form of natural religion and bring them in helplessness to the crucified Saviour and the Written Word. Intuitionalism has had its trial in the age now passing away, as Rationalism had in the previous one, and both have been found utterly insufficient."

"*The Intuitions of the mind, Inductively Investigated.*" By Rev. James Mc Cosh LL.D.

NOTE 6.

As illustrative of the shifting character of the solutions, offered from time to time, of the profoundest questions in metaphysics, take those worked out in immediate succession by Kant, Fichte, Schelling, and Hegel—names foremost among the most brilliant in the long series of speculative thinkers reaching from ancient times down to the present.

Kant claimed as the result of his reasoning that the real in its ultimate sense could not be an object of consciousness, that it is impossible to bring the object itself within the grasp of the subject. Fichte and the others accepted the conclusion and undertook to meet the requirement by constructing a philosophy of the real that should be above consciousness, *i. e.* "to expand the subject to the immensity of the object,"—an attempt which, as Dean Mansel affirms, "necessarily ended in the identification and consequent annihilation of both." Fichte worked out the ego and non-ego as entities beyond consciousness. Consciousness might authorize the inference *that* they are, but could not possibly inform us *what* they are, which amounted only to saying that the subjects or causes of sensible or intellectual phenomena are unknown. The effect of his scheme was to leave no room for the distinct existence of Deity and to resolve God into the moral order of things. After Kant and Fichte, and partly as the result of their systems, it was found that the Real could not become an object of science unless in some way it could be "immediately given or revealed to intelligence." There must be an absolute Knowing to answer to the absolute Being. Not only must the object of Knowledge be beyond consciousness, but it must be grasped by a faculty above consciousness. This was the problem which Schelling and Hegel proposed to themselves. It grew up out of the antecedent thought. The necessity cornered them. They attempted to meet it in two ways, Schelling by a direct beholding or intuition lifted above the conditions of time and space, Hegel by a logical reason equally lifted above the laws of thought, and so independent of them as to make consciousness not the substance, but the accident of thought. The results of both schemes are thus stated by Mansel, (Mansel's *Metaphysics*, pp. 312—14). With Schelling "subject and object are the same, both being merged in the absolute. The world of things and the world of thought are but two opposite aspects of one and the same being, manifesting itself without or with consciousness. The human reason is identical with the divine, and philosophy is not an imitation or repetition of the divine thought, but the divine thought itself developed into consciousness. The act of knowledge is an act of personal existence :—this is the testimony of the normal consciousness. The act of knowledge is also an act in which personal existence disappears in the absolute :—this is the testimony of the abnormal intuition. *Cogito, ergo sum*, says the one, *Cogito, ergo non sum*, says the other."

The system of Hegel also rests on the postulate of the identity of thought and being. "This assumed identity necessitates a conception of thought not only distinct from, but at variance with the evidence of consciousness. Thought according to the latter is manifested (so far as we know it) in relative, determinate, special states of my individual existence. Thought according to Hegel is an impersonal, indeterminate, absolute, universal, unconscious substance, becoming all things, constituting the essence of all things, and attaining to consciousness only in man. Creation does not imply a creator, nor thought a thinker. The Hegelian process may be described as a creation of the Deity no less than of the world, for it recognises no Deity apart from the world."

These characteristic speculations of Schelling and Hegel are by no means mere speculations. They long since emerged from their own abstract world into the world of living, thinking, believing, doubting men. They are influencing directly or indirectly thousands of thoughtful minds on many of the leading questions of the day. In most cases where any argument is attempted in defence of the grand postulate of Individualism—the mind the measure of all things, it will be found, if carefully analysed, that the argument is founded upon inferences drawn from these systems.

Note 7.

The *a priori* demonstrations here referred to are those built upon grounds outside of experience, *i. e.* independent of all mental or moral cognitions furnished by experience. They do not include therefore what are known as the

a priori demonstrations constructed by Newton and
Clark or by Des Cartes. In all these the fundamental
postulate, though originating in the intuitional consciousness, verified itself by experience and appealed in doing
so to the ordinary laws of belief and evidence. The
alleged failure of these not only did not prevent, but in
some degree encouraged the efforts of German thinkers
and of certain French and English writers who had
caught their spirit to elaborate arguments for the Divine
existence from ideas, which, when analysed, prove to be
little more than metaphysical abstractions in regard to
the nature of being that deserve to be classed among
the dreams rather than among the rational processes of
the mind.

NOTE 8.

The view here maintained finds not only a pertinent
illustration, but a strong confirmation—nay, an incontro-
vertible proof in the grounds of opposition to doctrinal
and historical Christianity assumed respectively by the
old Deism in England and the earlier Rationalism in
Germany, on the one hand; and by the later schools of
scepticism in both countries, on the other. The former
rejected Christianity both doctrinally and historically
considered, (1) because it contained doctrines repugnant
to the rational and moral instincts, and (2) because its
records contained miraculous attestations of such doctrines.
The doctrines could not be true because they violated

reason, and the history could not be true because it affirmed that miracles were wrought to prove them. The latter cordially accepts the doctrines because as spiritual ideas they are in harmony with reason, and adapted to the wants and instincts of humanity; but rejects the history because its miracles not only contradict the uniformity and immutability of nature's laws, but also because they were unnecessary and superfluous—the narrative of them having its origin in the wonder working, passionate desire of man to clothe with the marvellous whatever he has come to regard as divinely pure and great. These two theories based on the judgments of the moral reason or the moral and spiritual instincts are not mere variations of testimony. They are radically contradictory and mutually destructive. The antagonism is absolute and the inference is undeniable. Both schools agree in casting aside the history of Christianity as worthless and incredible, but for diametrically opposite reasons. Both schools perish in the conflict begotten of their hopeless disagreement;—the one denying Christian principles because the moral reason declares them incredible: the other accepting them because the moral reason sees in them the interpretation and fulfilment of its own profoundest yearnings. It only remains to be added that the later schools both in Germany and England rest their reputation for usefulness on the ground that they were chiefly instrumental in destroying the earlier.

NOTE 9.

Passing over many noteworthy signs of reaction in the higher thinking of England and the Continent from the bald, hard materialism that has of late years enlisted multitudes of disciples; I cannot forbear making brief mention of what is going on in the same direction in the best known circle of abstract thinkers in America. It is commonly supposed in the Old World that the American mind is either too busy with other things, or too undisciplined and immature, to be much interested in the great problems which have been the themes of the profoundest philosophic thought in every intellectually active age and among every people of ripe intelligence. The supposition is not borne out by the facts. Along-side and mingled with the ambitious energy and practical enterprise which have reclaimed a continent from savage wildness, and built up within its borders a new and powerful civilization, there has been, from small beginnings, a steady, though diversified advance in the cultivation of philosophy. The old arguments and inquiries touching the relations of subject and object, of the real and the phenomenal, of the sources and laws of knowledge, of the origin and government of the world, of the nature and destiny of man, of an intelligent First Cause and a Supreme Ruler, and all kindred themes have been re-examined, re-stated, expanded, modified, pushed to their logical inferences. How, and where, and by whom this kind of work has been done among us could not be told without entering into details in no way needful for the purpose of this note. In the summers of 1879 and 1880, in a quiet New England town, what has since taken upon itself, in a quite natural way, the name and work of a school of philosophy, assembled for conference among its leaders and for instruction of all comers. The teachers were of widely different antecedents and from parts of the country very remote from one another. They were drawn together simply as seekers after truth—as candid inquirers who had given much previous study to the subjects that were to engage them, and yet who had not gone far enough in their thinking to make definite theories or systems a rational necessity, or even a mental gratification. Some of them had graduated in the school of Utilitarianism, some in the best known varieties of the Rationalistic school ; while others had hovered on the verge, if they had not gone down into the depths of Pantheistic idealism, bifurcating, on the one hand into a worshipful estimate of reason and, on the other, into a transcendental type of mysticism. Generally speaking, the gathering was composed of men who had tried every school and were, on one ground or another, satisfied with none. They neither intended nor attempted to found a new philosophy. The only aim publicly avowed was to see what could be done to rescue philosophy on the one side, from the cold, careless, creedless, Godless grasp of the materialism which has been aptly called "the dirt," or, at best, "tadpole" theory of humanity ; and on the other, to

13

purge it of the scepticism built up on a spiritual or mystical basis. United in this one purpose, each teacher or discourser took his own line, and gave the results of his own studies, without stepping aside to review or to controvert those of his fellows. In this way nearly all the great thinkers of the past found a voice and an interpretation toned by what is characteristic of the deeper thought of to-day. Now the one most significant thing in this, for many reasons, very remarkable movement was, with rare exceptions, a strong, earnest tendency toward what, on the whole, may be best described as a revived and modified Platonism: *i.e.* a conception of the universe which makes matter the least part of it, which finds the supernatural above, beneath and around nature, which sees abundant room for the exercise of will-power divine and human amid all the uniformities and immutabilities of physical laws, which maintains that this world is not the world that rational beings believe it to be without a living, personal God at its head, which declares that man is what he is because the image of God is upon his soul and because an immortal life awaits him.

The first meeting of this Concord School excited only a transient curiosity. It was noticed by the public press and in intellectual circles as the whim of a few restless minds. The second, however, attracted wide and respectful attention, by its evident earnestness and sincerity of purpose, by its comprehensive range of subjects, and, quite as much, by the versatile and disciplined faculty for abstract thinking exhibited in most of its discussions. Though it arrived at no positive results of any appreciable value, and propounded no formulated philosophical creed, the wisest observers of the signs of the times generally regard it as a new and most hopeful departure in philosophy, and as the best reasoned and most powerful protest of the day against the grossly materialistic tendencies of recent scientific and metaphysical inquiry. As such it has been deemed worthy of this formal mention: as such, too, we may see in it a sign and promise of a time not far distant, when the deepest, most carefully reasoned thought in physical science and in metaphysics will be no longer, as now, the enemy, but the friend and helper of Historical Christianity.

Note 10.

Certain phases of modern thought have reached their present conclusions in regard to the nature and obligations of marriage, and also in regard to the grounds for its dissolution by easy and natural stages. Those conclusions are not of recent or of sudden growth, though the practical effect of them has only of late begun really to startle the well wishers and defenders of the purity and order of society. What wonder that an increasing number of men and women should see no sacredness in the marriage tie, and should contract it "unadvisedly and lightly," not "soberly and in the fear of God:" or that they should claim to be the final judges of the reasons and grounds of divorce, when, for centuries, both the common law and statute law of the English speaking race have held marriage to be merely and altogether a civil contract, and therefore a purely human institution, having neither a divine origin nor any formally divine sanction. What wonder that a relation which may be entered into without priest, minister, or magistrate, and even without witnesses, ratified and declared by no public or formal ceremony whatever—the consent of the contracting parties being alone essential to the validity of the contract, and this consent given according to the taste or judgment of the parties;— what wonder, I say, that the million should find no difficulty in concluding that a relation so formed may as easily and as lightly be broken asunder? Modern law itself, as interpreted by the best judicial authorities, is the parent of some of the worst theories and practices that now trouble us; and our Courts of divorce, by a righteous Nemesis, are beginning to tremble at the retribution which themselves have invited.

And yet the responsibility lies further back—even in what Society and the State themselves authorized to be done some three hundred years ago. It is sad to think that they could find no better way to redress the wrongs inflicted by a corrupt and perverse ecclesiastical guardianship of marriage anterior to the Reformation, than that of stripping marriage of all Divine sanction and Sacramental significance, and resolving it into what it is to-day. It requires no prophet to foretell the trouble and disaster, the moral impurity and moral decay that, sooner or later, will avenge the violated sanctity of this primary institution of God. In tracing to the Reformation the change which has been generally accepted both as to the conception of marriage and as to the proper mode of solemnizing it, it should be remembered that it was the political, not the religious element in the Reformation that originated the change; and that in this, as in many other things, even the Reformed Catholic Church was no match for what were deemed the necessities or the expediencies of the State. The Roman Catholic Church has been censured, justly too, for many errors and corruptions; but in this matter of marriage, she deserves honourable mention for the resolute, unflinching courage with which, in our own time, she has resisted the downward tendency, and affirmed over and over that she would discipline any of her members who ignored the authority of her sanction in a matter so inseparably connected with the law of God.

It is certain that the majority of persons in every one of our Christian communities are quite ignorant of what the Civil law teaches and rules as to what is essential to the validity of marriage; and while treating the subject, though only in this passing way, I have thought that it would not be amiss to append the following statements, taken from an article published recently in one of the ablest and best known of American Journals..........They—(enlightened people)—look upon marriage not as a sacrament, or in any sense a divine institution, as did the generations of the past; but consider it a mere civil contract, that may be completed by the consent of the parties alone. On this point Shelford says : "Marriage is considered in every country as a contract, and may be defined to be a contract according to the form prescribed by law, by which a man and woman, capable of entering into such a contract, mutually engage with each other to live their whole lives together in the state of union which ought to exist between a husband and his wife." Bishop says : "Marriage is a contract having its origin in the law of nature antecedent to all human institutions, but adopted by political society, and charged thereby with various civil obligations. It is founded on mutual consent, which is the essence of all contracts, and is entered into by two persons of different sexes, with a view to their mutual comfort and support, and for the procreation of children." And Lord Robertson, a Scotch Judge, remarks : "Marriage is a contract *sui generis*, and differing in some respects from all other contracts, so that the rules of law applicable in expounding and enforcing other contracts may not apply to this. The contract of marriage is the most important of human transactions. It is the basis of the whole fabric of civilized society. The status of marriage is *juris gentium* and the foundation of it, like all other contracts, rests on the consent of the parties ; but it differs from all other contracts in this, that the rights, obligations, and duties arising therefrom are not left entirely to be regulated by the agreements of parties, but are, to a certain extent, matters of municipal regulation." The learned Bouvier, speaking of the common law of England on this subject, says : " Marriage is a personal relation existing between a man and a woman, founded upon a civil contract, in which the assent of the parties is alone essential to ·its validity. All persons are able to contract marriage unless they are under the legal age or otherwise incapacitated. The age of consent at common law is 14 in males and 12 in females. The parties must be each willing to marry the other. No particular form of words or ceremony is required. Mutual consent to the relation of husband and wife is all that is necessary."

The law of the state of New York on this subject is well expounded by Judge Harris, who, in a case reported in the fourth of N. Y. Reports, page 230, says : " A valid marriage may exist without any formal solemnization. By the ancient common law of England, marriage, being regarded as a sacrament, must, to be valid, have been celebrated *in facie ecclesiæ*. But since the Reformation it has been uniformly regarded as a civil contract. In this State the common law rule exists, and whatever may be thought of its wisdom, the existence of the marriage contract is a fact which may be proved like any fact. The sanctions with which religion has invested this contract are not a matter of civil cognizance." And Justice Gilbert, of the Supreme Court in the case of Van Tuyl against Van Tuyl, in 57 N. Y. R., page 253, says : " A valid marriage, to all intents and purposes, is established by proof of an actual contract, *per verba de presenti*, between persons capable of contracting, to take each other for husband and wife. No solemnization or other formality, apart from the agreement itself, is necessary. Nor is it essential to the validity of the contract that it should be made before a witness." The most curious case that has ever risen under the laws of this State was the case of Bissell against Bissell, reported in fifty-fifth Barbour, page 355, which came up for adjudication before Justice Barnard a few years since. In that case a man and woman being engaged to be married, the former stated to the latter that he did not believe in marriage ceremonies, and wished her to waive the ceremony, saying that a marriage without it would be perfectly valid. She finally consented to waive the ceremony, and fixed the day for the marriage. On that day, while they were riding together in a carriage, he placed a ring upon her finger, saying : "This is your wedding ring ; we are married." She received the ring as a wedding ring. He then said ; "We are married just as much as Charles is to his wife, (referring to his brother and his sister-in-law). I will live with you and take care of you all the days of my life as my wife." She assented to this, and they went to a house where he had previously engaged board for "himself and wife," where they lived together for some time. In this case Justice Barnard held that it constituted a valid marriage. And in delivering his opinion in the case, he laid down the law as follows : "In this State marriage is a civil contract, and no religious form or ceremony of any kind is essential to its validity. All that is requisite is that the parties should be capable of contracting, and that they should actually contract to be man and wife. An agreement made in the present tense, whereby the parties assume toward each other the marital relation, is an actual marriage. This agreement may be either written or verbal, with or without witnesses, and may be proved like any other contract."

That eminent and learned jurist, Lord Mansfield, says: "If a man and woman seriously and sincerely enter into the marriage contract without the interposition of a clergyman or any religious ceremony whatever, it will be a good marriage by the law of God, of nature, and of the land."

Note 11.

I have assumed that the State or the Nation which is the concrete form of the State is not only a political but a moral organism; and further that is not only a moral organism, but that it has the essential attributes and functions of moral personality. I have ventured upon the assumption with a full knowledge of its liability to be called in question. There is much of the thinking of the time that assumes almost the exact opposite. On so grave a subject it may not be well to rest in an assumption followed by no proof of its reality. I find the (attempted) proof ready at hand in a work which, for some reason aside from its deep thoughtfulness, has failed to attract the attention which it deserves, ("The Nation,"

E. Mulford. 1872. Cambridge : Riverside Press pp. 16, 17, 18), "The nation is a moral organism. In the necessary elements of its existence in history it transcends the merely physical conditions of a physical organism ; and in freedom, and law, and order, in the fulfilment of a conscious purpose and vocation, and in the obligation to law are the very elements of a moral being. Its members are persons who subsist in it in relations which presuppose the personality of the members. There is in it the assertion of a justice which is the affirmation of a person in the recognition of these relations between the moral whole and the moral parts of the whole. Its law is regulative of the whole and of the parts, in these relations. It is as a moral organism that the nation is the sphere of the individual person—of the growth and formation of his character. It presumes an existence in a conscious relationship, and its fulfilment in the relations of a moral order. It is thus that there is formed in the nation the consciousness of the relationship of humanity and the moral life of the individual is apprehended in it as the life which is truly human.

The process of the nation is only as a moral organism. It is constituted in the order of a moral world. Its course is defined in law, and in law as prescribing the actions and relations of men as moral agents.

The conditions of history presume the being of the nation as a moral organism. History is not a succession of separate events and actions, but a development in a moral order, and in the unity and continuity of a life which moves on unceasingly. But it is only as the nation is an organism that this unity and continuity are manifest in it, and as a moral organism that this moral order is confirmed in it. The nation, therefore, cannot be comprehended in the definition, in its logical limitations, of a physical organism. The distinction of a physical and a moral organism is necessary as serving to illustrate the being of the nation in its necessary conception.

The physical organism is determined in itself by a law of necessity, as the tree which cannot be other than it is; the ethical organism is determined in a law of freedom which is the condition of moral action. In the physical organism each member exists only in its relation to the whole, as, for instance, the hand is nothing without the body, and has no separate significance; in the ethical, each member has in itself a necessary significance, and each member, furthermore, has the destination in itself for which the whole exists, and which the whole has in itself. The whole subsists in the same relation and has the same destination as the individual, and neither the whole nor the individual has a secondary existence, nor can be made only a means to the end of another. In the physical, the elements which are atomic, are taken up and separated again, and as they pass back into unformed nature, it is only to reappear in other and manifold forms; in the ethical the members are individuals existing each in his own identity, and each is so related to the whole that instead of a construction after the exclusive type of the whole, it is indifferent to say that the individual has his type in the whole, or the whole its type in the individual. But, further, the nation is a moral personality. This is determined in its consciousness and in this consciousness, subsists its independence of other nations. It is not to be necessarily what they are, nor as they are. Its object is before it, which it knows as its own; its freedom is in the working out of its vocation.

The condition of the realization of personality is the same in the nation as in the individual. This condition in each is the clearness and fulness in which it comprehends its purpose and in the faithfulness with which it works after the type of its own individuality. Again the nation is a moral person, since it is called as a power in the coming of that kingdom in which there is the moral government of the world, and in whose completion there is the goal of history. It is a power in the moral conflict and conquest which is borne through history. It is a power manifest in the judgment of history. But in the formal and artificial conception of the nation this becomes a fiction, and in the mechanical conception it has no moral ground. The nation is a moral person, since its development is in an integral moral life. Its character is its own, it is not derivative from any powers on earth; it does not proceed from them, and its responsibility cannot be transferred, nor its obligation rendered to them. As it has its own vocation and is judged in it, so it must have its own end.

Again, the being of the nation as a moral person has its witness in the consciousness of men. It has awakened the higher moral emotion and its response has been from the higher moral spirit. It has called forth the willing sacrifice of those who were worthy. The life of the individual has been given for the life of the nation. If the nation had only a formal existence, this moral spirit could have no justification, and if its origin was in self-interest, to call for self-sacrifice would be the negative of it; and if its end was only the protection of the life and property of the individual, this surrender of them would be the immediate defeat of its end. Again, the nation is a moral person, since it is the organized life of society, and society is formed in the spirit and in the power of a personal life. It is to be governed in the conscious determination of the will and to act as one who looks before and after. Its strength is in rectitude of thought and will; wisdom and courage, stedfastness and reverence, faith and hope are attributes of it, the highest personal elements become its elements and are moulded in its spirit.

Finally, the relation of the individual to the nation presumes, as its necessary condition, the existence of the nation as a moral person. The individual becomes a person in the nation, and this involves the existence of the nation as a person; for personality, as it is formed in relations, can subsist only in an organic and moral relationship—a life which has an universal end."

NOTE 12.

John G. Whittier, who has written some of the most tender and beautiful lyrics of the time and is regarded as one of .the most gifted and thoughtful minds in America, is generally accepted there as an able and moderate representative of the more advanced school of Individualism in religion and politics. Very recently he expressed himself in these words*.

" Everything valuable to the soul has its corresponding need in the soul. *Authority as a ground and element of Religion must wholly disappear.* The teachings of Christianity will be *on the needs of man*, and the claims for Christ will be based on the perfect character of his life and teachings, and not on His authority"; (i.e. as claiming to be the Son of God —essentially divine). " In these periods of transition all remedies must prove their adaptation to our needs by satisfying the demands of our reason and our spiritual wants"; i.e. it is of no moment that they are offered to us on the warrant of Revelation. They will be true only to the extent that reason affirms them to be so. The necessary inference from this is that there is little room and less necessity for the offices of faith.

* New York Daily Times, Oct. 4th, 1880.

CAMBRIDGE: PRINTED BY C. J. CLAY, M.A. AT THE UNIVERSITY PRESS.

www.ingramcontent.com/pod-product-compliance
Lightning Source LLC
Chambersburg PA
CBHW030823270326
41928CB00007B/871